PETER CRAVEN

THE WIZARD OF BALANCE

PETER CRAVEN

THE WIZARD OF BALANCE

BRIAN BURFORD

TEMPUS

This book is dedicated to the memory of Peter Craven, and also to all the riders, past and present, junior and professional, who have risked their lives and limbs on the world's speedway tracks.

Heroes die young, but they never fade away.
- Waysted (Way/Chapman)

First published 2003

Tempus Publishing Limited
The Mill, Brimscombe Port,
Stroud, Gloucestershire, GL5 2QG

© Brian Burford, 2003

The right of Brian Burford to be identified as the Author
of this work has been asserted in accordance with the
Copyrights, Designs and Patents Act 1988.

British Library Cataloguing in Publication Data.
A catalogue record for this book is available from the British Library.

ISBN 0 7524 2856 X

Typesetting and origination by Tempus Publishing Limited
Printed in Great Britain by Midway Colour Print, Wiltshire

CONTENTS

ACKNOWLEDGEMENTS

I would like express my thanks to Brenda and Leon Leat and the Craven family, Robert, Joan, Harry and Sheila Naylor, for their much appreciated help and blessing for this book. A thank you too, to all the ex-riders, mechanics, journalists, managers and historians for their assistance. But I would like to single out some others for a special mention: the late Frank Maclean, whose articles about speedway racing in the North West were an invaluable source of information; Cyril J. Hart of the Fleet News Agency for his contribution and loan of photos; David Blinston and Tony Mann for their help with, and recollections of, cycle speedway and the Aces; Peter Collins, Charlie Oates, John Chaplin, Peter Williams, my long-time buddy, Gareth Owen, Vic White of the Veteran Speedway Riders' Association, Nick Barber for his continued help and interest, Howard Jones of Speed-Away Promotions, Phil Handel for once again coming up trumps with his computer knowledge, Ken Smith for the loan of his programmes and books, Peter Jackson for supplying the statistics, and once again thanks to my mother, whose support has never wavered. To all the staff at Tempus Publishing a special thank you for continuing to support the sport of speedway racing. And finally thanks to Sam, Kelly, Shawn and Billy for their inspiration.

PREFACE

by Brenda Leat (formerly Brenda Craven)

When I was first informed that a book was being planned about Peter, I thought it was a wonderful idea as I feel sure readers will find his story both interesting and inspirational. I first met Peter casually when my sister and I used to go to the Ainsdale beach to watch the local novices practising at a training school run by Charlie Oates. We later met again at a dance hall in 1950 when we started going out together.

Although Peter achieved great success in his speedway career, he was always a modest man and was never changed by the fame he enjoyed. He always found time to talk to his many fans and sign their autograph books no matter how long it took. On a personal level he was always kind, thoughtful and loving to our children, and me. He enjoyed nothing more than being able to spend time together doing the things we all enjoyed.

I think my most memorable recollection of Peter's career was of him winning his first World Championship in 1955. At that time, while we all knew he had a good chance, his success was most unexpected, particularly as the media at the time gave him no chance of winning at all! This made Peter all the more determined to do well, and we were all ecstatic when he won the trophy. Peter loved his speedway racing, and when he raced it was just like watching poetry in motion. He was called the 'Wizard of Balance' because of his style and 'The Mighty Atom' because he was so small. I used to go and watch him as often as I could, and it was a very proud and wonderful time when Peter won the two World Championships at Wembley. He was wearing his British race-jacket, and when they played the national anthem, it was a very proud time for the whole family.

For myself, my treasured memories are of our wedding day on 17 October 1956, and the birth of our two children, Robert and Julie. His untimely death, on 24 September 1963, was a devastating blow to me, his children, and his family, and also to his many friends and supporters. Our only consolation is that he has been so well remembered, and revered by so many people for forty years.

I think that it speaks volumes for Peter's popularity that his fellow riders – now members of the Veteran Speedway Riders' Association and in particular Reg Fearman – have done so much during these last few years to keep his memory alive. Three years ago the VSRA, in conjunction with the Edinburgh Corporation, provided a plaque in Peter's memory which is now situated in the new Meadowbank Stadium in Edinburgh. This year, the 40th anniversary of his death, a memorial service is being organised by the VSRA to be held at the Liverpool Anglican Cathedral on 20 September 2003.

It's really nice that so many speedway supporters still remember Peter for the great rider that he was, and also for being a genuinely warm and caring person. I'm sure Peter would be pleased that he is so fondly remembered by so many people, and he would be quietly proud of a book appearing about him.

FOREWORD

by Peter Collins MBE (1976 World Champion)

Peter Craven was a big influence on my career, and he was the main reason why I chose to become a speedway rider. He was unbelievable and made such an impression that, just by watching him ride, he was such an inspiration that he definitely left a mark on me. He inspired me to enter speedway racing and try to emulate his achievements.

I was eight years old when I first went to Belle Vue Speedway, and I went every Saturday – I never missed it. Peter had already won the World Championship at the time, and he was the top rider there. He was so spectacular and so exciting that, as a World Champion, he was a massive influence.

I was brought up on a farm, and my father adapted a motorcycle for me to ride around the fields. In the yard we had a small cinder area that my friends and I would slide our bicycles around. Of course we always pretended to be speedway riders, and I was *always* Peter Craven.

My son, Chris, used to race for Buxton in the Conference League and there was another young lad in the team called James Wright. He is the grandson of Jim Yacoby, who used to race with Peter for the Aces. I am absolutely spellbound by the stories and the memories that he has of Peter. I am always keen to hear these stories and find out as much as I can about him.

The biggest regret that I have in my speedway life is that I never had the opportunity to meet Peter. However, I did get his autograph once. Belle Vue used to let some of the kids into the pits after the meeting and I waited for him to come out of the dressing room. Dick Fisher came out first, and then it was Craven and he signed the back of my programme – I still have it somewhere. As my own speedway career developed, I have become friends with some of the top riders of that time like Barry Briggs, Ove Fundin, Bjorn Knutsson and Ronnie Moore; I have got to know them. I would have liked to have had the opportunity to get to know Craven in the same way – but it wasn't to be.

Through my association with Belle Vue Speedway, both as a rider and as a promoter, I've met his widow, Brenda, and the rest of the family on a number of occasions. She presented me with the trophy when I won the Peter Craven Memorial. And then when I was the promoter and we staged the memorial meeting, I was stood on the centre green with her. But I have always found it difficult. I can't really explain why, but how do you converse with someone who was closely related to a person whom I admired so much? I suppose I was in awe of her a little bit, because of her husband and the inspiration he was in my career.

He had many nicknames and 'The Wizard of Balance' is one that readily comes to mind. He was so spectacular to watch. Most of the riders at that time were big left-leg-out riders like Clive Featherby, Clive Hitch and so on, and they would form a kind of tripod with the bike. But Peter wasn't like that; he relied on his balance and he used to have his head under the handlebars and, if he put his left foot down at all, it was often right up next to the engine. No doubt his lack of height was a big factor behind his exciting style, but he was so thrilling to watch.

At the time there were only a few riders of a similar style, like Billy Bales, Sonny Dewhurst – who I think only had second-half rides – and Soren Sjosten. But Sjosten was a bit taller. Later there were a lot more riders who were able to rely on their balance, like myself and Chris Morton, but the tracks and the machinery now allow a rider to race with more finesse. It was a lot harder in those days, and Peter was the pioneer of that style of riding.

I remember seeing the Golden Helmet match races with Ove Fundin. Fundin would wear the yellow Norwich race-jacket with the green star, and he was totally different in style to Craven. He would hug the inside line and leave Peter to storm around the outside, and they would pass and re-pass each other all the time. I also remember the handicap racing that involved the top five riders of that period. And even with a 20-yard handicap, Craven would be past the other three riders and into the lead by the time he came out of the second bend! He was so small, and he had so much natural talent and speed that you didn't know if he was going to go under them, around them or even over the top of them.

There are a lot of similarities between myself and Craven: we both raced for the same team, we both have the same initials – PC – and we come from roughly the same area. Comparisons were often made between us during my career. I was lucky enough to win one World Championship and I nearly did it a second time, but I can imagine how Peter had to change as a person to race a speedway bike and win races. I think we were both very determined like that once we were on a race-track.

I think I saw him at his peak. When he won the World Championship for the second time, I remember him coming to Belle Vue with the winged wheel World Championship trophy. But he didn't have the opportunities that I had. I don't think he had the team-mates around him to support him, and the sport was structured differently then. It changed when I started racing, and I was lucky enough to ride during a boom time for speedway in the 1970s. There were more Test matches, pair's championships and all these other competitions to race in that were not around during Craven's era.

I don't think we saw the best of him, there was still a lot more to come, but I would certainly put him among the top six riders of all time. Peter Craven was an extraordinary rider and he was something special – a real speedway hero.

INTRODUCTION

Speedway racing is a dangerous business, but the risks are put to the back of our minds during the thrill of competition. As the champagne flows to toast another success, the element of danger appears nothing more than a cautionary footnote. Nonetheless, when a rider does pay the ultimate price, its effect upon the sport and all who are associated with it can be devastating. The fall-out from such a tragedy is especially felt in a sport which takes pride in its celebrated family atmosphere.

British speedway was plunged into darkness when its favourite son died following a crash at Edinburgh on 24 September 1963. England's Peter Craven, the double World Champion, was a natural racer, and was the original 'Wizard of Balance' – so called because of his incredible balance on board a 500cc speedway bike. He was not only one of Britain's best ever riders, he was an all-time great. He spent the majority of his career racing for the famous Belle Vue Aces in Manchester, and was just twenty-nine years old when he was killed. He was cut down in his prime – while he may have lost his World title to Ove Fundin just ten days earlier, it seemed that his ability to regain the crown was well within his capabilities.

Although a speedway supporter for more years than I'd care to admit, I never had the privilege of seeing Peter Craven in action, but I knew all about him. In 1981, there was much interest and expectation when his son, Robert, appeared in second-half races at Swindon. Then the American, Kelly Moran, had his style likened to that of the great Craven and he was also called 'The Wizard of Balance'. In fact, their styles are of an uncanny similarity – especially when one takes into consideration the differences to track surfaces and engines. From then on, as the years passed, my interest in Craven has grown. It was an interest which eventually led to me contributing an article about the former Belle Vue rider for a magazine titled *Best of British* in 1996.

Sadly, Craven isn't the only rider to have lost his life while in the pursuit of glory on the world's speedway tracks and, inevitably, he won't be the last. But he was certainly a rider with one of the highest profiles. At the time, death on the world's speedway circuits – or indeed any kind of motor-racing circuit – was a regular, but unwelcome, occurrence. In some ways the danger aspect only added to the romanticism of the sport, and it was argued that a rider like Craven, a twice World Champion who possessed supreme ability, would not pay the ultimate price because of his great talent. His death shot down that theory in bright, blazing flames for all to see, and its aftermath smouldered for years to come.

Happily, such tragedies are less frequent in modern times. But, as with all motor sports where the object of the exercise is to be the fastest, danger and potential misfortune are never far away. No matter how many improvements are made to enhance the riders' safety, the competitors will always push the limits to be first.

So, just how dangerous is speedway when compared with other forms of motor sport? Benfield Sports International, who hold the marketing rights for the Speedway Grand Prix, promotes the high risk element by using the slogan: 'no brakes, no gears, and no fear'. Following the serious injury sustained by Denmark's triple World Champion, Erik Gundersen, during the 1989 World Team Cup Final at Bradford, the safety aspect was called into question by the national press as it had been a particularly bad year for injuries. Martin Brundle, the former Formula One driver who is now a television commentator, went on record in the *Daily Express* to describe it as the most dangerous of all motor sports, and also called into the question the riders' sanity! Sweden's all-round motorcyclist and World Finalist, Olle Nygren, described the art of speedway racing as 'staying away from the safety fence'. However, with the arrival of the air fence at Grand Prix level – and at a less than satisfactory number of tracks in the various leagues in Britain – this has set new standards in safety which can only be of benefit for the riders.

The bikes themselves are speed machines in their most basic form. But the sport is often derided by the naïve and uninitiated, who will often scoff at the mention of no brakes by replying: 'That's because they don't go fast enough to need brakes!' In an excellent book entitled *Speedway: An Introduction to the World of Oval Racing* by Alasdair Domhnullach, the author covers all forms of oval racing whether it is bikes or cars. He provides perhaps the best description in recent times of a speedway machine, and its often underrated, but powerful grunt.

The speedway bike itself is probably the purest and most basic racing machine that there is. It has a clutch and a throttle, but no gears, no brakes, and no rear suspension, and its purpose-built frame houses a single cylinder, four stroke, methanol burning 500cc racing engine. It has a tremendous power-to-weight ratio. It looks mean and menacing, and leaves you in no doubt as to its purpose.

Speedway has been likened to chariot racing from the days of the Roman Empire. Fans of the classic Oscar-winning film *Ben Hur* will find that speedway racing may contain the same competitive edge but, thankfully, not quite the same degree of ruthlessness. I do believe, however, that it takes a special kind of person to race a speedway machine and to be able to do so at the highest level does not imply insanity, but just an outlook on life which is different to our own. Craven was one of those 'special' people; in fact, as far England is concerned, none have been quite so unique.

Peter Craven was without doubt one of the all-time greats, and his death robbed the world of one of the most exciting racers in the long history of the sport. Even now, his fellow riders and supporters talk fondly about Peter, as there is still a lot of affection felt for the little Belle Vue superstar. For his family, it has not been pain free to recall the old times, but through their memories Peter's spirit still burns brightly. They have been nothing less than co-operative and this book would not have been the same without their encouragement. Indeed, such is the degree of love and care felt by all who knew him, that it is a testimony to Peter's character that he touched so many during his short life.

One

TALENT IN THE SANDS

Peter Theodore Craven was born in Liverpool on 21 June 1934 at the Oxford Street Maternity Hospital. He was one of twin boys, but sadly the other twin – who was christened Paul – died when he was three and a half years old. Nonetheless, Peter was part of a large and very close family that consisted of an older brother, Brian, and two older sisters, Pat and Sheila, and they were followed by two more children, Sylvia and Dinky. Their parents were Ben and Edna, who always encouraged and supported their children in their various interests and activities.

The Craven family lived in the Prestbury Road part of the city, which is situated to the east of the Liverpool – not far from the main road that leads to the Manchester. They came from the proud traditions of all families in Northern England, in that they were hard working and carved out a living through hard graft. This could not have been easy when the Great Depression of the 1930s hit home, but they were fighters and gallantly carried on as best as they could. This was a quality that probably served Peter well when he sat upon a speedway machine for the first time. His father, Ben, was by trade a Master Window Cleaner, who would employ others to assist on his rounds.

As is the tradition with all twins, Peter and Paul were very close, and they would share all kinds of things with each other. For example, if one of the boys received a sweet or a biscuit from a kindly neighbour, then the recipient would share this with his brother or acquire a second treat for his sibling. Their sister, Sheila, later recalled that they also shared a three-wheeled bicycle. Paul was the more outgoing of the two, but Peter, even at this early age, already displayed a quiet, unassuming personality that masked his subtle determination to succeed. That is not to say that he didn't possess a good sense of humour, because he did. He had a cheeky, impish quality about him, and his sense of fun and laughter would often mask his dedication to the task in hand.

It was also thought that if Paul had lived, he could have been the family's third speedway rider. Even at that very young age he was already showing signs of having great control when sliding a bike around. Paul passed away shortly before January 1938 from diphtheria, which was a great tragedy for the family. However, as the Cravens were such a close-knit family – a strong bond which still exists today – this helped them all to cope with the inevitable heartbreak.

Peter Craven attended the Ranworth Square Primary School and then moved up to the Abbotsford Road Senior School before attending the Walton Technical College. All through his education he quietly went about his business in a modest but effective way. It was a mark of his personality that he would always help others, and would do so in an understated manner. Years later, not only would he take this quality with him into adulthood, but also into speedway racing too. To this day, his family are still coming across people who will enthusiastically recount a story about when the Belle Vue star went out of his way to help them overcome a problem. And this would not always be racing related, as he would often help stranded supporters too. One of these stranded individuals was Leon Leat, who was one of Peter's closest friends and would later become his helper in the pits.

I had travelled to Leicester to see Belle Vue race, but I had mis-timed my train home. This was in 1953 and he gave me a lift home, and that's how I got to know him. Peter would always help people, and I was very grateful on that particular night.

When Peter was born the sport of speedway, or dirt-track racing as it was known then, was in its infancy. The first officially recognised speedway meeting to take place in Britain was at King's Oak, High

Beech in Essex on 19 February 1928. A massive crowd assembled to view this new form of motorcycle racing which had already taken Australia, and to a lesser extent America, by storm. It was organised by the secretary of the Ilford Motor Cycle Club, Jack Hill-Bailey. In the booklet *A Fistful of Twistgrip* by John Chaplin (published in 1995), its author tells the full story of the birth of the sport in Great Britain. It contains many pictures, including a photograph which shows the crowds assembled on the infield as well as around the perimeter of the track. *Motorcycle Magazine* said of that day: 'A day's sport as has never been seen in England,' and the *Daily Mirror* newspaper put a photographic spread on their front page.

However, there are historians who dispute the High Beech claim as the birthplace of speedway racing in Britain. There is evidence that confirms that racing on an oval circuit did in fact appear on these shores for the first time in June 1927 in Droylsden near Manchester. In 1996 the *Vintage Speedway Magazine* and *5-One* both ran stories about the claim that dirt-track racing was actually born in Northern England, some six months prior to the Hill-Bailey-promoted event at High Beech. If more evidence is required, then a report of the results appeared in *Motor Cycling Magazine* dated 30 June 1927. Riders like Charlie 'Ginger' Pashley and Freddie Fearnley successfully appeared at the event and would later race for the Manchester teams of that time: Belle Vue and White City. Therefore, their claim does seem to hold some credibility, and cannot be dismissed as another example of the old North and South rivalry.

It would appear that the definition of what constitutes to be speedway, or dirt-track racing of that period, has meant that Droylsden's claim has been dismissed because it doesn't quite adhere to the criteria. Experts and officials say that the circuit was not big enough to correspond with what was deemed to be a speedway track. Nonetheless, there are two things that one can learn from this pioneering dispute: firstly that speedway in the North-West was well established; and secondly that Craven was born into an area where he would have found it difficult to ignore the sport.

From that enthusiastic beginning, the sport soon began to expand and by the following year league racing was under way. Furthermore, the sport's first major individual championship was also launched and was sponsored by a London newspaper, the *Star*. It was therefore called the Star Riders Trophy in its first staging in 1929, but would later become known as the Star Championship. It was the forerunner to the World Championship competition which was officially launched in 1936.

The Championship went through a period of experimenting with different formats ranging from match races which were similar to the Golden Helmet of the post-war years, to the preferred method of sixteen riders, run over twenty races – the traditional system to determine individual tournaments until the 1990s. There were a number of reasons why the decision was taken to experiment with these different systems, but no doubt the overriding one was that speedway was just trying to establish a winning formula for both the riders and the public alike.

During its first year the English riders were not considered to be good enough to compete against the Australians and the Americans, and the Championship was consequently split into two sections: overseas and English. Australian Frank Arthur won the overseas section while Roger Frogley defeated the legendary Jack Parker to win the English section. The following year the English riders were allowed to compete against their foreign counterparts. However, it wasn't until 1932 when Eric Langton – who would later play a part in the development of Craven at Belle Vue – became the first English rider to win the Championship. His success was followed by fellow countrymen Tom Farndon, Parker and Frank Charles, before the launch of the World Championship brought the competition to an end.

Liverpool has a fine sporting history, and it is not surprising that the city was at the beginning of the development of speedway racing. But its history here is not one in keeping with the sporting traditions of the city. Liverpool staged speedway at Stanley Stadium on the Prescot Road, but there has also been racing at the Seaforth Greyhound Stadium on the other side of the city.

In 1929 a speedway league was introduced and the northern tracks of that time organised a competition that was sponsored by the *Sunday Chronicle*. It was titled the English Dirt Track League, but was often referred to as the Northern League because it was dominated by tracks situated in the north. It was a more appropriate name, and it was adopted as the official title during its second year of operation. Meanwhile, the southern clubs ran their own league too, but in the north many of the clubs failed to complete their fixtures.

After operating on an open licence at Stanley in 1928, Liverpool entered a team in the English Dirt Track League and finished in seventh place out of eleven teams – the Championship was won by Leeds which included Eric Langton in their side. The following season they did much better in the Northern League with a third place behind their Manchester rivals, Belle Vue and White City.

However, the Wall Street crash of 1929 triggered off the Great Depression which soon began to make its presence felt in Britain. This was possibly one of the main reasons behind Liverpool's closure after their 1930 campaign, although the venue re-opened in 1936 to take part in the Provincial League. Unfortunately, they experienced a mediocre season, but as they won as many matches as they had lost, it appeared that the team displayed some potential for the following year. But after a promising start the crowds dwindled and, financially speaking, it became impossible to continue to run at Stanley. Belle Vue's manager, Mr Eric Oswald Spence, stepped in and moved the team to their Hyde Road circuit and they completed their fixtures as the 'Merseysiders'. Given the rivalry between the two cities, this must have been a bitter pill for the Liverpudlians to swallow.

But it was the death of Oliver Hart's brother, Stan, which shocked the Chads' faithful and crowds dwindled. Stan died in a match at Birmingham when it was reported that his rear tyre had burst and the riders behind were unable to avoid him. Their last match was against Norwich on 30 October, and this marked the end of the Belle Vue Merseysiders.

As well as that spectacular exponent in the art of leg trailing, Oliver Hart, other riders to appear for the Liverpool team during those formative and turbulent pre-war years were Ginger Lees – who finished third in the 1934 Star Championship – Les Wotton and another set of brothers Ernie and Allan Butler. Eric Blain was another pioneering track legend who pulled on the Merseyside's race-jacket, and was also the captain. He recounted an alarming incident to Ron Hoare in his book, *Speedway Panorama*, which illustrated why spectators enter 'at their own risk'. He was racing at Belle Vue in a Jubilee Cup meeting when his engine blew to smithereens. He recalled that:

Bits of metal were flying around like shrapnel. A piece of the cylinder head wall struck a pillar in the stands right in front of the heads of a number of spectators. Undoubtedly, the pillar saved them from a very serious injury.

Frank Maclean, who would become one of Peter's closest friends and a sports journalist, saw his first meeting at Liverpool in 1937 and left a painful impression upon Oliver Hart. In his *Speedway Star* column, Maclean would later recall that:

Oliver took a tumble in front of where I stood on the huge Prescot Road bend and I decided to help. In those days it was a simple matter of jumping over the wire fence and all went well until I landed on Oliver's outstretched hand – with startling results! The rider remarked that his simple fall had become a painful experience for him and could I remove myself from his hand – and the stadium – forever! He made several blistering comments before being hustled away to the ambulance room.

In contrast to Liverpool's fortunes, the Manchester Belle Vue Aces team became one of *the* teams to beat, and their Hyde Road track at the Zoological Gardens was regarded by many as one of the best racing tracks in the country. During the pre-war years the club won championships in 1930, 1931, 1933, 1934, 1935 and 1936, and also won the National Trophy from 1933 to 1937. Furthermore, the prestige of the club was further enhanced when they were regulars on the roster as one of the venues for the five-match Test series between

England and Australia. With riders like Eric Langton, Frank Varey and Bill Kitchen among others, they boasted a side that contained some of the great pre-war talents.

On 3 September 1939 Britain declared war on Germany, with the Prime Minister Neville Chamberlain announcing: 'This country is now at war with Germany. We are ready.' In line with other sports, speedway, and in particular the fourth staging of the World Championship at Wembley, was cancelled. The World Championship had been a big success since its inception in 1936, with the world's best 16 riders competing before sell-out crowds. Chamberlain's declaration of war came just four days before the staging of the World Final, and it is one of the sport's great frustrations that the Final was never held.

American Cordy Milne was leading the qualifiers with 8 bonus points, but England's Eric Langton and Bill Kitchen were close behind with 7 points – a total they shared with another US racer Wilbur Lamoreaux. With other riders like former champions Jack Milne and Lionel Van Praag, Vic Duggan, Jack Parker, Arthur Atkinson and Alec Statham, all among the frontrunners, it is little wonder that speedway fans found the Final a mouth-watering prospect. And with Langton and Kitchen nicely placed in joint second, it seemed that, potentially, Britain could have had its first World Champion. But, alas, it was not to be. And the Final that never was, continues to be debated over a beer or two in the various bars around the speedway world with the eternal question: who would have won the 1939 World title?

Liverpool is situated on the bank of the River Mersey estuary, and it is one of the largest cities in England. Following the development of the Lancashire cotton industry, it established itself as one of the most important cities of the industrial age. But it is also one of the country's most valuable sea ports for Atlantic trade – a role that included the dubious distinction of providing a passage for the slave trade during the eighteenth century. During the Second World War, the city was of vital strategic importance in the war effort, and a major target for Germany's air force, the *Luftwaffe*. In the bitter and deadly war of the Atlantic Ocean, the city was a victim of Germany's relentless bombing campaign, whose aim it was to cut off the vital supply routes that were coming across the Atlantic. In so doing, Nazi Germany tried to restrict not only Britain's defensive capabilities, but also to apply further pressure on the country's already struggling economy. Liverpool also played another important role in the war of the Atlantic, when in 1941 the Prime Minister, Winston Churchill, persuaded the Admiralty to establish a Western Approaches Command Centre at Derby House on the waterfront. This task took on a more significant role when the USA entered the conflict.

Due to the heavy bombardment from the German air force, the port of London was closed indefinitely. Subsequently, the importance of the port at the Mersey meant that the *Luftwaffe* turned their attentions to this city with some devastating results. On eight successive nights in May 1941, the Germans attacked the city and killed nearly 4,000 people and over 180,000 homes were either damaged or destroyed. Peter's future wife, Brenda, recalled that it wasn't long after that that she was evacuated to a relative in Wales. She also remembered that there were fires raging all around the area.

Happily for the Cravens, the heavy bombing experienced by the docklands area and the centre of the city did not worry them quite so much, as they were situated far enough away from the location where the intense bombing took place. Sheila Naylor, Peter's older sister, recalled that only a few incendiary devices dropped in their area, although they always made good use of the air raid shelters. It was common practice during those days for the children of these targeted cities to be evacuated to safer places in the countryside, but because of their location, Peter and his brother and sisters were spared from an unwanted stay in a rural area.

Peter was a small child in stature, which was a characteristic that he would carry with him into his adult life. He always looked younger than his age, but his youthful appearance didn't always work in his favour. But just as his understated personality hid a determination to succeed, so his lack of stature masked an inner strength that surprised anyone who didn't know him.

Sheila recalled that as a family they would all cycle to Formby for a much-needed break from the stresses and strains of wartime Britain, and for little Peter his lack of stature did cause some concern for his mother on such a journey.

We all used to cycle ride to Formby and we had second-hand bikes in those days because of the war. However, my parents always made sure that we all had bikes. But my mother would worry about Peter because she thought he would get tired. My father used to have a rope, and when he started to tire, he would attach the rope to his bicycle and then pull him along! So when my mother would mention this to my father, he would always say that he had the rope with him if it became too much for him! I think he was about ten years old then. Anyway, as tired as we all were, when we got a few miles away from our home, my father used to make us all race for the last few miles. It became very competitive for the honour of being the first member of the family to get home. Well, I can remember Peter's little legs going round as fast as they could, as even at that age he was very determined.

Nearby Manchester also suffered air raids because of its importance as an industrial city. Furthermore, the establishment of the Manchester Ship Canal in 1894, which provided a link to the Mersey estuary, made the city another important target for the German bombers.

It has been a mark of the war that the people of Britain courageously carried on their daily lives as best they could, despite the backdrop of the constant threat of air raids and rationing. All the big cities in particular suffered massive attacks and destruction, but the Belle Vue Speedway Club was the only track in the country to operate race meetings throughout the hostilities. Southampton, West Ham, Crystal Palace and White City (Glasgow), ran meetings during the early years of the war, but as the situation grew more serious, only Belle Vue managed to continue and justly proclaimed: 'We never closed.'

With many of the sport's riders engaged in doing their duty, the riders who appeared in these meetings grew less and less as the war progressed. Most of the meetings were either individual or pairs championships – although there were some team matches. On many occasions nobody really knew who would be riding until the very last minute. When you consider the situation that the country was in at this time, it is quite remarkable that a sufficient number of riders managed to be present to put on their regular Saturday meetings, but somehow there were always enough participants.

There were other obstacles to overcome because of the restrictions on petrol and other fuels during this period. Under the rules of rationing, petrol was not to be used for pleasure, and the Belle Vue management issued a statement in the programme stating that 'no petrol whatsoever was used'. The bikes were run on a wood alcohol substitute, and the contents of the riders' tank were tested regularly. As the war progressed, spare parts for the bikes also became scarce and their prices rocketed as a result; while tyres were made to last many more meetings than they normally would have. Just as the public were being as resourceful as they could by having to make do and mend, so too did the riders at the Manchester track. In fact, it was said that the riders and mechanics during the war years became very ingenious when it came to putting together a machine that was competitive – these were skills which would serve them well after the hostilities had come to an end.

Among the riders to appear were the Aces regulars Frank Varey, Bill Kitchen, Oliver Hart and Eric Langton. Other racers such as Tommy Price of Wembley, West Ham's Eric Chitty, Alec Statham and Norman Parker also rode at Hyde Road. And even some of the boys that were in the services, like Australian Bill Longley and Denmark's Morian Hansen, made appearances when they could. The premier event of this period was the British Individual Championship, which West Ham's Canadian star Eric Chitty won three years in succession from 1940 to 1942. His run of success was ended by Ron Clarke, who would go on to achieve great distinction in the post-war years as the captain of Odsal (Bradford). Frank Varey won the 1944 event and Bill Kitchen was the victor in 1945.

Varey had retired on the eve of the 1936 season, but he was tempted back to race during the war years. In a series of articles that appeared in the *Vintage Speedway Magazine* titled, *El Diablo Rojo – The Frank Varey Story,* its author, Dick Bott, carried this revealing quote of speedway racing at Belle Vue during this time:

It helped to keep speedway going at Belle Vue and we ran all through the war to terrific crowds. That wasn't surprising, of course, because the servicemen and women were allowed in free and there were thousands of them in the Manchester area. We were paid a straight ten quid a week during wartime, but we weren't in it for the money. We were simply glad to be able to provide some form of entertainment. Many of the service people who came to watch had been very badly injured and it was heartbreaking to see them.

As the war ended in 1945, more tracks staged meetings and the sport began to wind itself up for a revival in the following year. Freddie Mockford took speedway back to London, and he revived the London Riders' Championship which Ron Johnson won at New Cross. However, the first meeting at New Cross was the Victory Cup which was won by Jack Parker. Sheffield and Middlesbrough also re-opened before the year was out, and Johnnie Hoskins revived the sport at Odsal – with the help of Eric Langton – while White City (Glasgow) also roared to the sound of speedway engines again. Preliminary rounds of the British Championship were held at both Newcastle and Odsal, and the British Championship was staged at Belle Vue and was won by Bill Kitchen.

With a new season to plan for, the sport was indeed back. This was undoubtedly due to the efforts of Mr Eric O. Spence, the Belle Vue boss, and his speedway manager, Alice Hart. Not only did they manage to keep speedway's home fires burning during the turbulent war years, but by doing so the sport had a platform from which to build a rapid revival. One wonders if the sport would have recovered so well if it hadn't been for the Aces' management's stubborn refusal not to let the war disrupt their plans.

Alice Hart's hard work was rewarded when she was appointed onto the Belle Vue board. Speedway racing is predominately a man's world.

For a woman to be successful in a managerial role was as rare as bananas were during this time! However, there were female racers during the pre-war years, most notably Fay Taylour. She possessed talent of a sufficient standard so that she was able to compete against the male stars of that era. Nonetheless, it was the auburn-haired Hart who was regarded as the 'First Lady of Speedway'. She also combined with Frank Varey to guide Sheffield Speedway when they re-opened after the war, and she was also involved in the Edinburgh promotion too.

Hart was also instrumental in beginning the speedway schools, and also introducing novice races to the programme that were designed to find new talent. With Harold Jackson also involved in the process of discovering new stars for the Aces' post-war teams, it seemed that the club were likely to carry on where they left off before the outbreak of the Second World War.

Everyone connected with British speedway was optimistic that the 1946 season would be a success, but no one really expected the public to flock to the tracks in such numbers. Rationing was still in place and the country was struggling to cope with the re-building process. However, the public were in the mood for escapism; escape from the daily grind of immediate post-war Britain, and from the horrific images of the war which were still fresh in their minds. There was no television to speak of in those days, so speedway racing offered all the thrills and spills, and the heroes and villains, that the public were craving for. Furthermore, the public were eager to get out and enjoy themselves after spending so long behind blackout curtains.

The return of league speedway was a massive success, with nearly seven million people paying to attend meetings that year. 80,000 people turned out to see a league match between Wembley and West Ham at the Empire Stadium – the promoters of today would bite your hand off for half of that total for a league meeting. But the season wasn't without its controversy. The riders threatened to strike if the controversial grading system was not scrapped, as they were not happy with the different pay scales that were in place for each grade. Needless to say, with massive crowds hungry for speedway action, a settlement was quickly agreed.

Belle Vue won both the National Trophy and the ACU Cup, and provided the league's top scorer in Jack Parker – who also finished the year as British Match Race Champion. But the National League Championship went to the booming Wembley Lions, with the Aces finishing in the runners-up position.

However, the aftermath of the war meant that the World Championship was not resumed until 1949. This was because many of the pre-war riders were still serving in the armed forces and were waiting to be demobbed. Furthermore, many of the foreign and Commonwealth riders had returned home during the war. Therefore it was decided to stage an alternative meeting which was sponsored by the *Sunday Dispatch,* called the British Riders' Championship. It was contested by riders from both the two leagues of that period, and a series of qualifying rounds took place until there were just sixteen left for the Final at Wembley. Tommy Price won the first staging, and he was followed by Jack Parker. The only foreign rider to win the event was an Australian, Vic Duggan, who won the title during its final year of operation in 1948.

Perhaps the best indication of just how popular speedway racing was back then can be denoted by the fact that a film based upon the sport was released in 1949, *Once a Jolly Swagman.* Among its stars were Dirk Bogarde and Sid James, as well as two future stars of the long-running BBC television comedy series, *Last of the Summer Wine*, Bill Owen and Thora Hird.

The film was based on a little-known novel of the same title by Montagu Slater, and told the story of Bill Fox (Bogarde) and his rise from a factory worker to a speedway star. The racing sequences were performed by riders such as New Cross skipper Ron Johnson, and Ron Howes of Rayleigh. Some of the scenes were actually filmed at the New Cross stadium, but at Pinewood Studios, now famous as the home of the James Bond films, they constructed a replica track for close-up shots that consisted of a straight, a bend and floodlights. They also recreated the New Cross pits area at Pinewood with breathtaking attention to detail.

When it comes to the glamorous world of film-making, it's not often that motorcycle racing is used as the basis of a plot for a potential block-buster. And this was especially so in the Forties. Therefore, a member of public could be forgiven for the following incident which was reported in the *Speedway Gazette* in its edition dated 4 December 1948.

Director Jack Lee and his production team were carrying out a night shoot for the racing scenes, when to the amazement of the film crew, a fire engine roared its way through the gates of the studio. A local resident had seen the glare of the lights shining from the replica track and alerted the local fire service that a raging fire was ablaze somewhere within the studio complex! Happily the crew all saw the amusing side of the incident, and they were able to continue filming. For this unidentified individual at least, the speedway boom had yet to reach the doors of his Buckinghamshire home.

In spite of the success that speedway racing was enjoying, the film didn't trouble the box office too much. Critics all agreed that the racing sequences were of an excellent quality, but the movie sank without a trace. However, it remains a cult classic among speedway fans, and it is still the only *bona fide* big screen movie to appear about the sport.

Quite apart from its speedway connection, there is another reason why this film warrants inclusion in this book: and that is that Craven was a big movie fan. It has been well documented that 'The Wizard of Balance' would go off and watch a film before a major meeting like the World Final. It was his way of relaxing before an evening's racing, and while he was watching the film he could immerse himself in the plot on the big screen before preparing himself for the task ahead. But, significantly as it turned out, Brenda revealed that she can remember watching *Swagman* with Peter at the cinema, and recalled that he enjoyed the drama of it all. When you consider that the release of the film coincided with his own persistant beginnings in the sport, one can only speculate about the measure of influence it may have had on him.

Peter enjoyed most types of films but he especially liked the fantasy musical, *Carousel*. It was released in 1956 and starred Gordon Macrae and Shirley Jones. The plot evolved around Macrae's character, Billy, coming down from heaven for one day in an attempt to make amends for the mistakes that he had made during his life. It was considered to be something different from some of the more light-hearted musicals that were doing the rounds at the time. This film left quite an impression upon him; so much so in fact that he named his second child Julie after the character portrayed in the movie by Jones.

As well as making trips to the flicks he also enjoyed cinematography, and, along with most people from the Merseyside area, he also followed football too. In fact, his long-time friend and pits helper, Leon Leat, would later recall that when he wasn't racing he didn't spend his time discussing speedway, but the fortunes of the football teams and other everyday things instead. As a young lad growing up in a city with two of the finest football clubs in the country, it was not surprising that he took a keen interest in the sport. His family recalled that he would wear the big studded football boots of that period, which probably appeared even larger on a young Peter because of his slight frame. Nonetheless, the legacy of his interest in football was that he would continue to follow the fortunes of Liverpool FC.

As his speedway career developed, Peter was able to use the training facilities provided by Liverpool FC – thanks to Bill Shankly, with whom Peter was on friendly terms. He also made good use of their physiotherapy department to assist with the injuries he picked up during the course of his racing career. He could see the benefits that regular training could have on his career, and he was carrying this out at a time when the average sportsman's fitness levels were a far cry from what we come to expect today.

The boom in speedway racing at this time meant that new clubs were springing up all over the kingdom. Attention once again turned to Liverpool – which was still regarded as one of speedway's sleeping giants, despite its less than successful flirt with the sport on two occasions before the war. A promoter from the pioneering days, Jimmy Baxter, began to look at suitable venues to re-introduce the sport to the city.

Baxter was one of the men who were responsible for the introduction of team racing in 1929. It was a move which brought an end to the circus-style shows of that period, and brought professionalism into the sport. It was felt that if anyone could make a success of the sport in Liverpool, then it would be the experienced, pipe-smoking Baxter. Significantly, he had already established speedway at both Plymouth and Southampton which, of course, were both sea ports.

He viewed several venues in the area, including the greyhound stadiums at Seaforth and Breck Park. However, both were deemed unsuitable. New Brighton was huge as it was a cycling track, but it lacked the facilities. At the last minute, Baxter decided to revive the sport at Stanley Stadium. It had all of the requirements he was looking for: a railway station that was close to Prescot Road, several bus routes passed by the entrance, and there were enough people living within walking distance to make it a viable proposition.

Baxter brought some of his staff with him from his Southern Speedway Company, the most notable of whom was former rider Gordon Parkins. He came north from Plymouth, found a house in the area and was installed as the track manager. Baxter realised how important it was to include the local people as much as possible. Hector Chipchase was responsible for the organisation of the Seaforth track during its occasional spells of racing activity, and he was brought in as the team manager. Phil Hughes, who was an ex-rider from the 1928 days, was the coach; he combined this role with his other duties as the assistant team manager. The programmes were printed in the city and he also used local tradesman to help with the construction duties. Baxter's use of local people and facilities was designed to build awareness of the re-opening of Liverpool Speedway, and also to help establish local pride in their club.

The track was 446 yards in length and consisted of long straights and narrow bends. A lot of care went into the building of the track, as the bends had brand-new bricks carefully laid into its base. The top dressing was lovingly sprinkled, shovel by shovel, around its length.

The team's nickname was the Chads, which was a fictitious propaganda war-time character who would always be depicted as peering over a wall. They entered the Third Division of the National League, and raced their first match against Stoke on 11 April 1949. Their starting team was captained by local star Harry Welch, and he was joined by former Plymouth rider Alex Gray, another local discovery Charlie Oates, Fred Wills, George Bason, Stan Bedford, Tom Turnham and Ernie Steers.

The new team lost their opening match 66–42 in a National Trophy encounter. But there was enough entertainment to encourage the locals to come back for more, and their gates averaged around 11,000. The Chads eventually finished in ninth place in a league which contained thirteen teams, and it appeared that the club had established itself in the city. Everyone knew about the Liverpool Chads!

The 1949 season seemed to represent the peak for this 'boom period' for speedway racing. It appeared that things couldn't get any better for British Speedway when the World Championship was revived, as British riders filled the top three places. Tommy Price was crowned Britain's first World Champion in front of a capacity crowd, reported to be 93,000 people. Jack Parker took the runners-up spot and Louis Lawson was third. Just to make sure that the world knew that Britain was best, Jack's brother, Norman, was fourth. In fact, British riders occupied all but one of the top seven places – veteran American Wilbur Lamoreaux was fifth. Never again would the British riders be so dominant in the World Championships.

With the British riders, and speedway racing in general, enjoying such a successful time, the various national newspapers of that period couldn't ignore the sport. Additionally, with Britain cleaning up in the World Championships, the sport's reporters were keen to inform their readers of the success that their country was enjoying – the *Sunday Dispatch* sponsored the World title now that the British Riders' championship had been dropped following the re-launch of the World event. Therefore, young men of a sporting and competitive nature – preferably with an interest in motorcycles – would have found much to draw their attention.

This was especially so for the Cravens, for both Peter and Brian had already displayed a keen interest in motorcycles – perhaps, with the benefit of hindsight, it was more than the usual interest that boys of that age would demonstrate. Among the supporters to make regular trips to Stanley to follow the Chads' fortunes were the Craven family. Naturally they became very interested in the Liverpool team, which had been revived from the ashes of the pre-war years and, under the guidance of the astute Baxter, they were expected to flourish. Speedway racing, with its massive crowds combined with an image of a glamorous motor sport that was accessible for the ordinary man with drive and ambition, soon began to appeal to the Craven boys.

It has always been a curious fact that the sport doesn't attract the regular biker type of individual in the crowds that road racing does – this is especially so during these modern times. Quite often new riders would not emerge from the similar Grass Track discipline, or another form of motorcycle racing, but from cycle speedway instead. It was quite normal for riders to 'move up' from the cycle version to try their hand at speedway without ever having ridden a motorcycle at all. It is a practice which is less frequent now, although the promising Premier League rider Lee Smethills has a successful pedal background that earned him a British title. However, with the exception of Craven, perhaps the most successful speedway racer to have dabbled with the cycle version was the five times World Long Track Champion and twice British Champion, Simon Wigg, who won the East Anglian Under 15 Cycle Speedway Championship.

Cycle speedway is exactly what is says: a bicycle version of speedway, but considerably slower! It is a minority sport, but it still survives in various parts of the country. Its fortunes are often mirrored by that of its motorised cousin: if speedway is popular and attracting good gates, then this will be reflected in the pedal version.

It was Peter and Brian who helped organise a cycle speedway club in a nearby area at Lower House Lane. The whole thing was influenced by their interest in the Liverpool Chads speedway team and, as a result, they called themselves the Prestbury Chads. This enthusiasm soon developed into a serious activity that attracted fascinated locals and the interest of speedway riders and supporters. However, the Prestbury team did actually appear in 1948, pre-dating the return of the Liverpool team by a year. This has been confirmed by Tony Mann who is the Secretary of the Bury Cycle Speedway team. Therefore, as speedway racing was attracting massive media attention at that time, it would seem likely that this group of lads organised this club through their own interest in speedway and, perhaps, Liverpool's link with the sport. But also in 1948, there was a training track that opened at the Ainsdale Sands which was a popular tourist attraction in the area – more about that later.

However, it was reported in the local press that Peter Craven was considered to be too small for a place in the Prestbury cycle team. 'You are too small. Grow up, Shorty, and we'll put you in the team,' it is quoted as saying. But he was not put off by this rejection, and instead he was determined to show them that they were wrong. He raced against rivals that were twice his size, and while he crashed a lot, his tenacity was there for all to see.

Frank Maclean was one of speedway's distinguished journalists, and he recalled his first sight of Peter on a bicycle in a booklet produced as a tribute shortly after his death, entitled: *Peter Craven: Tribute to a Great Little Champion – Edited by Ernie Hancock.* Peter was riding for their cycle speedway team in the city, and Frank's wife, Trudy, had seen this tiny tousled-haired young lad in action. She told her husband that she had seen someone who would make a good speedway rider.

We saw a small boy in a big green jersey and trousers worn with the continual sliding from a bike, riding against boys almost twice his size and more often than not getting the worst of it. But always coming back for more. Then one evening the Chads were in trouble. One heat to go and the star injured. Captain Harry Seekts put the tiny Craven in his place and after a hectic ride the Chads won the match.

Maclean would later recall that it was Peter's first cycle speedway race win and, despite the success he would later enjoy on a more powerful speedway bike, it was a win that he would always remember as one of his greatest victories. Afterwards Frank spoke to him, and he revealed his grand ambition: 'I talked to him and he told me that one day he was going to ride for Belle Vue.'

As a result of this meeting, Maclean and Peter developed a friendship which would last until Peter's death. But it was his wife, a former nurse who had met Maclean during the war, who first discovered a champion in the making. However, Peter's sister, Sheila, recalled that many recognised that Peter had a quiet determination about him. It was noted that Brian Craven was more of a showman and, perhaps, more colourful than his younger brother. But while he may have been more outgoing, it was wee Pete, the man they would soon call 'The Mighty Atom,' who was showing all the signs of real talent and an ability that was destined to be recognised on a worldwide scale. Nonetheless, Peter was looked upon as just another one of the lads, and no one realised that they had a future star in their midst.

There is no evidence to suggest that the Prestbury Chads were anything more than an amateur organisation that would race in a few challenge matches against local sides in the area. David Blinston, a life-long Belle Vue Aces supporter and former cycle speedway star who was also the manager of the England Cycle Speedway team, said that there is no record of the team being connected to any of the official cycle speedway governing bodies. Nonetheless, he said that there were many clubs of this nature in the region, and they would race on areas of wasteground that were often left derelict following the air raids during the war. Indeed, Blinston had his first taste of cycle speedway on a track that was built where two houses had once stood, but were destroyed by the German bombs.

When a person climbs to a level of great sporting success within his chosen field, there is always more than one individual who will claim that they discovered the person in question. And so it was with Peter Craven. What is likely is that those people, whose recollections follow, probably did discover – or see – Peter at different stages of his development for the first time.

His interest in speedway racing had grown and, accompanied by his parents, he made a journey to Halifax with the Liverpool Supporters' Club. He was particularly impressed with the riding from Chads' favourite, Charlie Oates, which led to a chance meeting that would determine Peter's path in life. It was a memorable meeting that Oates remembers fondly to this day.

I had been racing at Halifax, and it was a track that I always went well around. I always had a good night there, explained Oates. *The next day, I went to Victor Horsman in Pembrook Place to get some spare parts. The manager there was Bill Quinn, who was a great pal of mine. I was talking to Bill and there was this little kid who had his nose pressed up against the window of the shop. He was sat astride a cycle speedway bike. The next thing I knew was that I felt this tug on my sleeve, and I looked down and there was this little kid staring up at me with golden hair and brown eyes. He had a look of adoration in his eyes; it was like he was looking at God. And I said to him: 'What is it?' And he said that he saw me ride at Halifax as he had travelled with the Supporters' Club with his mum and dad, and would I sign his autograph book? So I did and he said: 'I leave school soon, can I come and work for you?' And that's how it all started. We made arrangements with his father and he came to work for me as the garage lad. We used to send him to places on a Bantam motorcycle to pick things up, and he worked for me until he was called up for National Service.*

Charlie and Peter developed a strong relationship, and it was noted that Charlie was a hero to the youngster. Later, when Craven was without doubt Britain's top rider and a World Champion, he would still make regular visits to Charlie's shop. But despite the success he was enjoying on the track, Oates said that, to him at least, he still remained 'the Garage Lad'. Therefore, it would seem that it was Charlie who influenced his career more than anyone else.

At this point, Brian too was keen to try his hand at sliding a brakeless 500cc, four-stroke speedway machine. There was a feeling that riding a cycle speedway bike was great fun, but they were keen to try the real thing. Their father was encouraged by the interest that his two sons were showing in this motorcycle sport, and set about acquiring a speedway machine to get them started.

In correspondence with the author, Brenda wrote that:

Peter came from a working-class family and, with quite a large family to support, money must have been quite tight for his mum and dad, Edna and Ben. However, his dad, as well as working during the day, also got a night-time job in order to save up and buy a speedway bike for his two sons.

As Brian was the eldest, he would be the first to benefit from this new machine. But, as Sheila revealed, Ben actually borrowed the money to buy them a bike. He took a second job at the famous Jacobs biscuit factory to repay the debt.

While their parents were being very supportive of their sons' new-found dreams of glory on the speedway tracks, not all were quite so happy. Older sister Sheila in particular was a little bit disappointed with her parents' support for her brothers' latest craze. She explained:

It sounds silly now, but I was a little bit annoyed that my marriage plans were put on hold because of Peter and Brian's interest in speedway. There was only so much money available, and I wasn't too happy that my plans and dates and things had to be put further forward into the future. My parents supported their interest in speedway, and my father could be a bit 'adventurous' shall we say.

The speedway bikes of the period were a lot different to the highly-tuned and fast projectiles that modern-day stars such as Tony Rickardsson and Jason Crump now push to the limits. During the pioneer and part of the pre-war years, the bikes and engines of choice were of a wide range. These could include the famous marque of the Harley Davidson, the Rudge or indeed the Douglas. More often than not, these bikes were adapted for speedway instead of being machines that were especially made for speedway racing. These all required a different technique, and that is probably one of the main reasons why there were so many variations of styles on display at an average speedway meeting in those days.

Naturally, technology moved on and it wasn't long before manufacturers began to produce machines designed specifically for competition on speedway tracks. These bikes have used methanol fuel since 1929, when petrol was dropped in favour of this alternative, which is also used in Champ Car racing and the Indy Racing League in the USA. this alcohol-based, colourless liquid burns faster than conventional petrol when near a naked flame, although it can be extinguished by water.

However, by 1930, a new breed of speedway engine was developed called the JAP. It was produced by J.A. Prestwich – the name 'JAP' being an acronym for the factory – who was more famous at the time for their road racing engines than anything else. But it became the dominant engine in the sport until the mid-1960s, when the Czechoslovakian Jawa machine emerged to become the engine of choice for the front runners. By 1949, not only did Britain have the best riders in the world, but also the best speedway engine too.

Therefore, it was a JAP engine that Ben Craven set about obtaining for his sons, as it was the *only* machine that any speedway rider of a serious nature just had to have. It was Liverpool's captain, Harry Welch, who supplied the bike and so the beginnings of a career on the oval speedway tracks began to beckon.

Brenda also believed that it was Welch who was among the first riders who saw Peter on a cycle speedway bike and recognised his potential, which would eventually lead to a trial for their speedway team. This is also a recollection that is shared by Peter's sister, Sheila.

What follows has become folklore within speedway circles: a tale of a tenacious and natural talent, whose stubborn determination to succeed has served as a lesson to all beginners and underlined his status as a true legend in the sport.

A day after his sixteenth birthday – 22 June 1950 – Peter went along to Stanley Stadium for his first taste of riding a speedway bike. He borrowed his brother's machine, and put in a few laps round the track before he promptly crashed into the fence and sustained concussion. In

Indy Car racing in the USA – where many races take place on very fast oval raceways called 'Super Speedways' – a rookie's progress is often coldly determined by this statement: 'There are two types of drivers: those who have hit the wall, and those who are going to.' Craven had just passed his first rite of passage as far as speedway development was concerned.

For a little while his enthusiasm was dampened by his crash into the Stanley safety fence. A clipping from the local press quoted him as saying, 'I'll never be able to handle a bike.' But his determination to be a Liverpool rider meant that he decided to turn to his mentor, Charlie Oates, and took part in his training schools on the Ainsdale Sands.

Meanwhile, his brother had displayed enough ability to make an occasional appearance as reserve for the Liverpool Chads during the 1950 season. His best performance was a 5-point return against their local rivals Fleetwood. I suspect that this drove Peter on, for as well as sharing the same interest in motorcycles and developing a taste for racing, they were also very close as brothers.

Joan Craven, who was married to Brian, lived at the opposite end of Prestbury Road, and used to watch the Prestbury Chads Cycle Speedway team. She recalled that they were very close indeed, and the brothers used to involve the whole family as much as they could.

They were exceptionally close, as they both loved their speedway racing. Brian would often help Peter in the pits, and travel together and all that. It was quite usual for Peter to arrive back from a meeting late at night, and we would hear a knock on the door, and it was Peter. That's what they were like, and they would discuss things at any hour to help each other. The Cravens are a very close-knit family and Mr Craven – we always called him Mr Craven even though we all knew his name was Ben – he was a lovely man. After you met him you soon realised why his sons, or indeed the rest of the family, were such nice people. There is so much warmth there, and even though my husband has now died I am still very much part of the family – it was the same for Brenda. So it's not surprising that Brian and Peter were so close, and speedway is, or it was then, a family sport. I remember we all used to go and watch the racing, and groups of families used to go along too.

Oates experienced a bad accident while appearing for the Chads in a league meeting at Swindon. The Robins rider, Danny Malone, crashed into the Liverpool favourite and Oates sustained a badly broken arm and a fractured skull. Unfortunately, these injuries would keep him out of serious speedway action for some years. The Speedway Control Board (SCB) at the time would not sanction his insurance, so he was in a position to help Peter develop his racing skills.

The Ainsdale Sands are situated on the Irish Sea coast, approximately five miles south of Southport. It was opened as a training track in 1948, but it was never officially recognised by the SCB – this hasn't prevented it from becoming one of the most famous of all training venues in the sport's history. Frank Maclean recalled in one of his many articles about the sport in the North West, that there used to be a notice on the Sands that read: 'Dirt-track racing is not permitted on the Sands'. And then contradicted itself with a notice alongside it which would read: 'Parking for training track 2s 6d.' Indeed the Southport Corporation used to do very well from remuneration received from novices parking their vehicles close to the sands. Furthermore it has other sporting links, as the triple-winning Grand National horse, Red Rum, had used the area for exercising and training, while the Sands are also associated with the land speed record attempts too.

Now it is a nature reserve and provides a habitat for many coastal and wading birds. The dunes are also home to the rare natterjack toad which has bred there since 1977. The Southport Corporation closed the facility as a training track in the early 1960s, but it played an important role in speedway racing in the North West.

It was Charlie Oates who first made use of Ainsdale to try out his bike, but he was prevented from doing so by the warden of the area.

The warden stopped me and said that I couldn't ride there. The foreshore belonged to the Ince Blundell Estate you see, so I went along and asked them about using the shore to practice on and they agreed, providing I paid a rent of one penny per year. We could only race there on a Sunday during the winter. And that's how it started. There were anti-invasion posts that were left there from the war, so we had to remove them to mark out a track. A gang of us got together and we had to dig down for nearly five feet to get these things out, and then break them up. But inside these things there was steel tubing, so we had to get the welder out and chop them up. We moved the debris to the edge and it formed a kind of seating area – or rather people adapted it for seating. Once the tide had gone out, it left a nice smooth surface on the sand, and it was good to race on. It used to cut up a bit as we went on, but it was all right.

At this venue a novice rider could learn the basics of riding a speedway bike. He could learn to lay down his machine safely, and also the nuts and bolts of caring for his equipment. Even after a novice had earned a place at a club, he could still enjoy assistance from the venue. The circuit was in use all year round – riders would often use the Sands to test components and set ups during the season, even though it was officially closed to bikes – and even when it was snowing you could still hear the roar from the bikes of dedicated and determined rookies.

We used to run training sessions and organise events on the Sands, Oates recalled. Peter came along and we used to get crowds of people there to watch. At one point we had 15 coaches there. We had riders from Halifax, Bradford Stoke, all over, and we used to get a lot of them there. Some would come to keep race fit, while others just wanted to try out their bikes. It was free, whereas some of the others like Rye House and so on, you had to pay. Frank Maclean used to do the programme and it was quite popular. Brian and Peter used to race there, but Peter used to be there every Sunday with Mr Craven. I had a lot of time and respect for Peter's father. Even when Peter was a top rider, he would still come to Ainsdale and help out and pass on advice to some of the riders. He was a natural. I could go well round tracks like Halifax and Exeter, but Peter could ride any track – and ride them well too.

While Peter and Brian were learning their trade, other members of the family took an interest. Ben Craven, although not mechanically minded, would always be there to help out with what he could. The whole family became involved, as Sheila recalled:

We used to have a lovely time there. Pat [the oldest sister] *used to make the flags to mark out the track in the sands. We used to get quite an audience. They were very happy times. Charlie Oates used to run it, and he was Peter's mentor really. He really looked up to him.*

Some of the ladies used to make cups of tea and go around selling them, so we could put a little bit back into the pot for the lads, Oates recalled. *Sometimes we would get a cup or something for them to race for – that sort of thing. We used to hold dances as well and some very good friends of mine, a Mr and Mrs Gillespie – who were speedway fans – used to help organise it. Mrs Gillespie was a professional confectioner so she used to make the cakes and they were lovely. Her daughter, Pam, she was well known for getting up on stage and dressing up in a top hat and tails, and doing a routine with a song and a cane. She used to do that at our dances, and she was very popular. Everyone used to help, and we had a great atmosphere and a lot of fun.*

Enthusiasm was the key to the success of the venue as a training facility, but this enthusiasm meant that they would often forget the time. On a few occasions, the participants had to make a mad dash for the road to save the riders and their equipment from being cut off by the tides! However, racing during the winter could be a hazardous experience at this location.

On one occasion Maclean, Peter Craven and the other riders found themselves at the mercy of thick fog and ice. Darkness had fallen swiftly, and due to the fog they could only see about a yard in front of them. It was bitterly cold and the cars were huddled together in a circle. There were around 20 or so vehicles there that included riders from Manchester and Bradford. No one seemed to know what to do, until Peter decided to make a move and a convoy of vehicles followed his lead. He wrapped himself up in all the scarves he could find, and hung his head out of the window to drive through the fog.

They passed Ainsdale Station and more vehicles tagged onto the end of the convoy. Peter, through a combination of endurance and courage, was leading them. And although their progress was painfully slow through open country, they were at least inching their way homeward. When they got to the perilous Ince Woods, the convoy stopped to allow stragglers to close up before continuing their journey to Liverpool. Peter was freezing cold, and the stop-start journey only made it an even more frosty experience for the future Ace, but they made it safely to the city. It was a memorable journey, but many of the party chose to remain in the city until the fog had cleared, as they didn't fancy their chances without the guidance and skill of Peter to lead them.

Of course the Sands were also a popular tourist location during the summer months, and the presence of the bikes seemed to add to its attraction. It was here that Brenda first met Peter, and a romance began to develop when they met again at a dance hall. But the natural beauty of the area was not lost on Peter and Charlie, as the latter explained:

At other times Peter and Brenda, and my wife and I, would go off into the dunes and have a little fire in the evening. Sometimes we would also go for a swim. They were very happy times.

At this point there were speedway clubs at Belle Vue, Liverpool, Fleetwood and sometimes at Wigan too. Therefore, Ainsdale was not the only popular venue for novices to go to. Ernie Appleby had constructed another training venue at Newton Heath on a disused tip, and Oliver Hart also had a training track at Coppull, approximately thirty miles north of Wigan, on which Cyril Cooper and Australian Dick Seers launched their careers.

Appleby was riding for Fleetwood when he crashed and injured his leg, which signalled the end of his riding days. Therefore he channelled his energies into constructing a 320-yard cinder track at this location in the Manchester area. However, it was advisable to exercise plenty of caution at the bottom bends, as an over slide could result in the rider hurtling down a steep slope! Furthermore, precious time could be spent regaining the riding surface.

The most notable product of this school was Peter Williams, who would later appear as a team-mate of Craven's at Belle Vue. He was also born in Liverpool and was a greengrocer's assistant. He used to use his half day on a Wednesday to practise his riding. he remembered that:

The track was rough at times, and big stones used to hurt your face and arms, but we used to ignore it all when Ernie and rider Cyril Cooper used to teach us the basics of the sport.

A rivalry began to develop between the two training venues which eventually resulted in the organisation in 1951 of an historic match. Halifax and Odsal boss, Bruce Booth, controlled the meetings that took place at both of the circuits. He also supplied the helmet colours and the flags. In some ways it was looked upon as an unofficial Liverpool versus Manchester encounter. Nonetheless, despite the snow flurries, an audience of 1,000 people saw the sand boys win both the encounters. It was Reg Wilson — a telephone engineer from Liverpool, and not be confused with his namesake who would later race for Sheffield with such distinction — who led the scores for the victors, while Frank Corrie was the Heath's top scorer. Newton had four team managers, Appleby, Cooper, Bill Dalton and Jack White; while the Sands also had a trio of their own in Charlie Oates, Stan Bradbon-Potter and a very young Peter Craven.

George Woodall, who would become Brian and Peter's future brother-in-law, was also on hand to help at Ainsdale, and he also rode there himself. He was a character, but his enthusiasm meant that he was always willing to lend a hand to help. Among some of the other riders to appear on the Sands was an intrepid character called Tommy Murphy.

Tommy was a bit of a clown, Oates recalled. He used to ride during the intervals at Liverpool with rockets and things strapped to his bike! What a character he was and he was afraid of nothing. He was ex-army, and during the war he won the Military Medal for bravery because he captured a German machine gun post single-handed. Only Tommy could do that, he was fearless. He was a big man, six-foot tall, blonde-haired and blue-eyed — a very handsome chap.

Under the watchful eye of Oates, Peter began to make some progress and also develop the beginnings of that exciting style of his. He was without doubt the most outstanding novice at Ainsdale, and the most famous product to emerge from the school.

I used to ride at the Sands, and ride up close to the riders to get them used to being close to other riders, explained Oates. *That was very important. Peter was a natural and he was up there with the rest of us almost straight away. At first he used to try and ride like me, but as he got more confident he began to develop his own style. I think it was at Belle Vue, after some tuition from Eric Langton, that he really developed that head under the handlebars style of his.*

With renewed confidence, it wasn't long before this tiny teenager was keen to display his progress to the bosses at Stanley Stadium, and hopefully win a place in the Chads team. In an article that is credited to Peter which appeared in the 31 October 1953 issue of *Speedway Star*, he revealed that Harry Welch suggested that he should try his luck at Stanley again.

While I was belting around the Sands, getting into all sorts of difficulties, and cutting every sort of caper there was to cut, unbeknown to me I was being watched by Harry Welch, who at the time was riding for Liverpool, wrote Peter. *Heaven knows what I did right but Harry suggested that the Liverpool management might be interested, why not go along and make a nuisance of myself.*

Therefore, he once again presented himself at the Liverpool track. He did one lap and hit the fence again! Despite this, they must have recognised his potential as he was given the opportunity to race for the Chads in their next fixture. Peter Craven was about to turn a wheel as a professional speedway rider at last. But his struggles were not over yet, and further advancement was required before he developed into the country's finest rider.

Two

INVENTING 'THE MIGHTY ATOM'

Peter Craven made his debut appearance for the Liverpool Chads in an away fixture at Leicester on 30 March 1951. He failed to score in a match that saw Leicester run away with an emphatic 61-23 victory over their north-west rivals.

He was not an overnight sensation and appeared for the Chads in only eight official matches that year. Craven raced in second-half events, and continued to test and practise at the Sands with Oates, combining this with his job at the Victor Horsman motorcycle shop.

Peter managed just 8 points in total that season, but he impressed everyone with his performance in a match against Ashfield (Glasgow). Liverpool beat the Tigers, but Peter scored 7 points that included a victory over the American Nick Nicolaides. Nicolaides was the captain of the USA side that took part in a Test series against an England 'C' team. Therefore it was a notable win and a triumph that underlined the potential that the teenaged Craven possessed.

His team-mates that year included established riders like Harry Welch, Len Read, George Newton and Reg Duval among others. But despite that experience, Liverpool was not encountering a particularly good season in the Second Division, and since re-opening they had always found themselves in the lower half of the league table. They eventually finished thirteenth out of sixteen teams that year, and the championship was won by Norwich.

Nonetheless, Peter's lack of stature created a spectacular style of racing, as he relied on his balance more than the standard method of the foot forward style. He was considered to be somewhat unconventional as there were only a few riders around who possessed a similar style of racing – although it would be a couple of years yet before he perfected the technique that would make him one of the most spectacular riders the sport has ever seen. However, he was dubbed 'the new Billy Bales'. Bales was another tiny racer who had performed well for Yarmouth before national service interrupted his progress. He returned to the top flight in 1952 with Norwich, and it was during his time with the Stars' team that he really established a name for himself.

Like Craven, Peter Williams was also in the early stages of his career. He was a product of the Newton Heath training track, and he used to travel to Stanley with Buck Whitby on a Monday night to watch the racing. He believes that it was George Newton's leg-trailing style that was at the bottom of Craven's own distinctive technique of riding.

Buck lived in Manchester and he used to come up to the training track at Newton Heath. He helped and encouraged me, and I would travel with him to Liverpool.

I have always thought that PC developed his style of riding from watching George Newton. George was a leg trailer and had tremendous balance. At this time, 1951/52, George was not a well man – I think he had tuberculosis – but his early rides could be breathtaking. Most leg trailers would sweep around the outside, and ride in the heaviest of dirt. Watching this at Liverpool, with its long straights and tight bends, really did produce the best of speedway, which is something that is lacking now.

However, I never really knew Peter that well at that time, although I probably rode against him in second halves. I can't remember anything other than I liked the track with long fast straights. You really had to know the bike to get round the tight bends.

Peter's lack of stature and his youthful good looks did not always work in his favour. It is a fact that he never looked his age, and as a result his sense of humour was often put the test. During a league match for the

Chads at Stoke, the man on the pit gate refused to allow Craven into the pits as he didn't believe that this tiny young lad could possibly have been old enough to ride as reserve for the Liverpool Speedway team. He refused to believe him, and told him to move along and let the other riders through. It wasn't long before he was missed, and the Liverpool team manager, Gordon Parkin, went out searching for him and found him in the queue outside the stadium with his 2s 6d ready to pay at the turnstiles!

The situation was repeated at Halifax, as once again the marshal refused entry to the little Liverpudlian. This time, however, Frank Maclean came to the rescue, and convinced the pits marshal that Peter Craven was indeed old enough to race and was a valuable member of the team. Eventually the gate was opened, and PC was allowed in to prepare for the evening's racing.

Peter kept his sense of humour and took it all in his stride. Brenda said that he would have liked to have been a bit taller, but nothing else bothered him. Of course, as his career progressed, all the pit gates across the land would be open for him as everyone would soon know who Peter Craven was.

During his formative years, the sport's press were quite interested in his lack of height and slight frame. His lack of inches, combined with the fact that the famous Aintree race course was situated near his home city, meant that he was often being compared with a race horse jockey. But he later revealed that he was most definitely only interested in the motorised description of horse power.

Despite my small build – 103lb fully stripped, 62 inches high, according to my Army record paper – I have never had any ambitions to be a jockey, he explained. *Give me a motorcycle every time. All my life, ever since I was knee high, not that much taller now, I've craved for a bike.*

The big story of that year though, was the decision of Jimmy Baxter to retire from the sport. Baxter complained about the crippling entertainment tax and the high prize money which meant that he closed his track at Southampton, but Liverpool was able to continue. In *Stenners 1952 Speedway Annual (World Edition)*, its contributor Len Simpson revealed the problems that the sport in Britain – in particular the Second Division - was now facing. His comments seem to confirm that the 'boom period' was over. He wrote:

Actually reduced entertainment levies and reduced riders pay still would not get some of these centres through another season. Cutting of expenses can represent for them no sweeping transfer from losses to gains – merely occasion a temporary reduction in losses. Their problem can be solved in one, and one only, fashion. The answer, not through decreases of expenditure, but increases of income: more people through the turnstiles.

Peter had proved that he had real ability and potential, and he was still only seventeen years old when the season ended. However, a heavy crash at Cradley Heath in May seemed to put the brakes on his progress, and he was out of the saddle for some 'considerable time'.

But he had plenty of time on his side to develop, and he found that he was very much part of the Chads' plans for 1952. He was listed in their squad of nine riders in the aforementioned *Stenners Annual*, and continued to practise at Ainsdale when he could. Charlie Oates recalled an incident that illustrated the drive and ambition that Peter possessed even at that early stage in his speedway career.

I recall on one occasion we had a visit from a children's radio programme. Peter was being interviewed and he told them that he was going to be World Champion. And I thought you cheeky little … but he knew what he wanted.

He was hopeful of making a real impact during his second season, but unfortunately this breakthrough didn't materialise. Peter found points hard to come by, and with the club struggling in the lower reaches of the table, it was becoming clear that they were losing their patience. He appeared in just five official fixtures for the Chads that season and scored a meagre 5 points, and worryingly he gained something of a reputation as a rider who crashed a lot. Nonetheless, it was obvious that he was struggling, but to the trained eye the potential was still there – it just needed something, or someone, to nurture and develop it.

While Peter may have been struggling on the track, he could still count on the support of his number one fan for encouragement – his future wife Brenda. In correspondence with the author she wrote:

I must say that I thought he was fantastic! When he was first discovered he rode extremely well – especially for a beginner, and he was hailed as the new Billy Bales. Unfortunately, after his initial success at Liverpool he suffered a loss of form.

Very few who stood on the terraces of Stanley Stadium would have believed the events that were about to unfold as they watched this tiny, impish little racer toiling away behind Second Division opposition for the odd point. It was hard to convince anyone that here was a future heat leader, never mind a future World Champion.

But when someone possesses such an abundance of natural ability, it is only a matter of time before that talent shines so brightly that the light will guide the disciples of speed to find it. Alan Morrey, who has been associated with Belle Vue Speedway for nearly sixty years, recognised the potential he displayed and recalled:

I used to be Alf Webster's mechanic, and he was riding for Liverpool at the time. I first saw Peter ride in second halves at Stanley as he was trying to break into the team there. He shot out of the gate and went into the first bend and he passed everyone while he was locked up – that was amazing.

Morrey began his long association with Belle Vue during the war years, and because so many of the staff had been called up to serve in the forces, he began attending to some of the jobs that were left vacant. He started off as the colour steward and, following encouragement from the rest of the management team, he was appointed Clerk of the Course in 1959.

I was Alice Hart's blue-eyed boy, he admitted. *For some reason she took to me. I told her that there were only two kids that I considered to be worth signing, and that was Brian Crutcher and Peter Craven.*

Crutcher was known as 'Nipper' and he made a massive impact during his formative years at Poole, and then he enjoyed further success as a member of the Wembley team. At the time many of the sport's pundits believed that he was destined to be England's next World Champion, and Craven and Crutcher were later locked in a battle to be the top British rider. Crutcher remembered:

I first encountered Peter at Liverpool in 1951. I was introduced to this young lad who was very small. He should have been a jockey, he was so small. But he was a really nice chap.

Peter Williams had already begun making second-half appearances at Belle Vue in 1952, when, after just a few weeks, he made everyone sit up and take notice. He progressed from his qualifying heat to the Final and finished in second place. Unfortunately, his progress was brought to a serious halt when he crashed and sustained a fractured skull. It was an injury that kept him out of the saddle for 17 months. He couldn't remember anything of the crash, but much later Ken Sharples told him that it was Split Waterman who had 'dumped him' and caused Williams to crash.

It seems possible that Williams' serious injury prompted the Belle Vue management team to look west to Liverpool for a replacement. Alice Hart and Jack Parker took in the action at Stanley, and showed a particular interest in the tiny young racer that Morrey had told them about.

After a promising start to his career he had lost his form and had made an appearance at Fleetwood. But he attracted the interest of Belle Vue – despite finishing last in all of his races when Parker and Hart were watching – and he had the opportunity to ride at Hyde Road for the famous Belle Vue Aces.

I always had a longing for Belle Vue, Peter later admitted in *Speedway Star, whether it was because they had the gardens which you could wander around after the meeting or not I do not know. But anyway, here were Belle Vue taking an interest in a pint-sized throw out from Liverpool.*

After the conclusion of a match, which was usually followed by a short interval, the second half of the programme was an individual tournament to determine the rider of the night. These races would consist of a series of scratch races and the winner of each race would progress to the winner-takes-all final. This was an ideal opportunity for the young riders to match themselves against the more experienced team members. It was also an opportunity to impress the bosses and stake a claim for a place in the team.

Jim Yacoby, who was one of Craven's team-mates at Hyde Road in the 1960s, also revealed that Belle Vue were one of the few clubs in the country that would put a lot of effort into nurturing new talent.

I progressed through the second halves at Belle Vue. I bought my first bike for £20. I think everyone wanted to ride at Belle Vue because it was the glamour club of speedway racing. It was the Manchester United of speedway clubs. It was also the only club with purpose-built workshops, and they would pay the riders who raced in the second half – and a lot of clubs didn't.

It was a productive formula that helped nurture and develop new talent. And it wasn't just at Belle Vue, but at other tracks as well. It was during one of these second-half races, which were called 'Bubble Bouncers', that the Aces' fans had their first glimpse of Peter. Among the crowd one evening was Tony Mann.

I first saw Peter Craven race in a second half at Belle Vue. I was in the bar, and we heard the noise of the engines and went outside to watch the race, and all I could see was this red helmet peering over the handlebars and the front wheel – and that was Peter Craven. He won the race and defeated Louis Lawson, who was a top rider in those days.

He made his league debut for Belle Vue in their home match against New Cross on 24 May 1952, but failed to score as the Aces defeated the Rangers 48-35. During that season he made a further five league appearances for the Aces, but scored just 3 points. It was clear that the step up from the Second Division to the top division in the National League was too soon for this all-action racer. But the Aces liked what they saw, and he officially joined them in 1953 on a free transfer from his local club – which turned out to be one of the best bargains in the history of British speedway.

There was much to learn and see at Belle Vue Speedway. They were the glamour club of the sport, and the track was acknowledged as one of the best in the country.

Belle Vue was the best race track in the country, agreed Morrey. *You could ride the inside, the middle, or around the boards, it was that good. We had a white wooden fence, and Ivan Mauger used to say that because it was white you could see it plainly and you could get right up into the dirt. The wire fences that they had at some of the other tracks you couldn't see so well at night. Vic Duggan used to say that if you couldn't ride Belle Vue, then you couldn't ride anywhere.*

The track was 382 metres (418 yards) in length, and the supporters were able to get very close to the riders as they whipped past on the straights as there was very little space that separated the track from the fans. The roar of speedway engines reverberating around the old wooden stadium is a sound that, once heard, is never forgotten. That soaring sound within the wooden beams of Hyde Road was just one of the many elements of speedway racing at Belle Vue that made the venue so special.

The stadium was situated within the grounds of the Zoological Amusement Gardens, and it was a booming place to visit. Speedway racing was just one of the entertainments that used to take place there; others included wrestling, a funfair, zoo, dance halls, gardens and later stock cars could also be seen roaring around the track. Peter Williams has vivid memories of the complex.

During my early years there, Belle Vue was almost a family-run business. The top man would often have a walk round and he was a real gentleman. He would ask: 'How are you this morning Pete?' That made for a very nice atmosphere, and I suppose Coventry might have been similar. But Belle Vue was a monster of a place when it was empty. If you walked through the grounds before the gates were opened, there would always be people cleaning the rides, mending, sweeping, painting, and so on. The whole place was special. When it was sold to Fortes, the accountants moved in. Belle Vue had for years catered for people who were looking for a cheap day out. Suddenly the price of a cup of tea had doubled, and I think that's when it started to go wrong. Later, of course, zoos became a dirty word and that ensured more problems.

The visiting speedway teams loved to come to Belle Vue. Harringay and Wimbledon with the likes of Barry Briggs, Ronnie Moore, Split Waterman, Cyril Maidment, Ron How, they couldn't wait to have a go on the rides and the big dipper after the meeting.

The old Belle Vue was a wooden stadium – all wood. I remember one night Tommy Price passed me on the back straight on the last lap, but then he tried to take me a bit deep on the pit bend, but I turned back underneath to beat him to the line. The thunder from the stamping of the feet on the wooden stands is something that I can still hear today. A pretty full Belle Vue would mean a crowd of 15,000 plus. Tommy Price, who had been a World Champion, was very gracious when he came over to compliment me. Things like that help to make you what you are.

The Aces team at that time included Jack Parker, Louis Lawson, Ken Sharples, Bob Duckworth and Ron Johnston among others. Parker was an established star and Lawson was a former World No.3. In 1951 the club had finished runner-up to Wembley in the First Division – as they had in both 1949 and 1950. But in 1952 their performances were not so consistent, and they slipped down the league leaving Wembley as the dominant team. Nonetheless there was a lot of experience on hand for the emerging riders to call upon both on and off the track.

Ken Wrench was an announcer at the stadium, and he revealed in a Summer 2000 edition of the *Vintage Speedway Magazine* that the experienced riders knew that the fourth bend could be useful for obscuring some form of villainy from the view of a less than experienced referee. The solid wooden fence would hide a part of the track if the referee was not aware of it. This had caused much confusion over the years, as sometimes innocent riders could suffer exclusion at the hands of a rider who was an experienced performer around Belle Vue.

Eric Langton was one of the legends of speedway racing and is also one of the club's all-time greats. Like many others, he could see the potential that Craven possessed, but he was one of the few who really was in a position to be able to help him. He took the young Craven under his wing, and from his guidance he slowly began to make some progress. Significantly, Langton developed a new 'Langton' frame for PC which was the key to his progress. He had been riding a frame from his good friend Charlie Oates, but while that may have been fine at the time, he now needed something more forgiving. PC paid for the bike in instalments on a weekly basis. Langton recalled that:

Peter had the ability to go into the corner faster than anyone else, but he had a flat spot in the middle of corners and we could never cure him of that. When he came to us he was far too set in his ways. We got him nowhere near as good as he could have been.

Craven later revealed that Langton had a lot to say about his riding:

Miss Hart gave me second-half bookings, and Eric Langton began coaching me, telling me all my faults, and believe me Eric had plenty to talk about. My faults went round the Belle Vue track more times than Johnnie Hoskins' best hat!

His speed into the corners probably accounts for why he began to struggle at Stanley. Peter Williams has already revealed that the long straights meant that you could certainly get the speed, but the short, tight turns meant that the rider had to turn very hard. If, as has been suggested by Langton and others that the frame he was using at that time was not the best choice for his style, then it is not surprising that his form dropped away during his early appearances for the Chads. Therefore, the wide open spaces of Belle Vue's Hyde Road stadium probably suited him more than Liverpool.

Peter Collins, who would succeed Craven at Belle Vue as one of the stars of the Seventies, agrees that Stanley probably didn't suit his style of riding at that stage of his career.

With that style of his I can see why he struggled at Liverpool. But once he came to Belle Vue, and the wide open spaces, well, he never looked back did he?

It seems that most people knew that he had the ability and the talent to make it, as Williams recalled:

I have always believed that Belle Vue thought that they had a star in the making in me, but when I got injured they cast the net and they brought in PC from Liverpool. Peter had a reputation for falling off at Liverpool, and his equipment wasn't very good. At Belle Vue we had an ace engine man, Bob Harrison, and two good frame men, Harold Jackson and Harold Gilchrist. There was no doubt that with Peter's easy style combined with riding reliable equipment he would soon get into the team. Peter rode in second halves at Liverpool with Sonny Dewhurst and I think Tommy Murphy. The other notable thing was that no one really came through from Newton Heath or Belle Vue for another few years.

However, in 1952 Peter was due to fulfil his national service obligations. It was the law that every man had to spend two years in the armed forces – a rule that was abolished in 1962. His brother, Brian, had already carried out his duty and had distinguished himself as a member of the Royal Signals Motorcycle Display team. Brenda revealed that Peter's arrival in the army was delayed because of a 'minor injury' he sustained while racing, so his conscription was deferred by three months – that took him nicely to the end of the season.

Peter carried out his basic training at Blackdown and Deepcut before he was posted at the Territorial Barracks at Stretford near Manchester. Fortunately he was able to continue his speedway career because his commanding officer, Lieutenant Colonel H.E. Hole, allowed him time off to race at Belle Vue.

As part of the 42nd Lancashire Infantry Division he spent most of his two years' national service as a batman driver to Lt-Col. Hole. In a letter that was passed on to the family shortly after his death, the officer recalled fondly his memories of Peter and his ability to handle speed.

Young Peter was really too small to drive and had to use a cushion beneath and behind him in order to reach the pedals. Despite this, he was without doubt the finest driver I found anywhere on three continents and the nicest batman who ever served me. In the 42nd Division his driving was a byword; I have met few drivers who could hit any corner or curve in the road at such a high speed, and take it without the slightest alteration to his steering. His driving was always impeccable and his road manners a delight.

There are many things I remember about him – the look on his very shy face when, shortly after becoming my batman, he fitted new rank badges and collar dogs to my 'blues' and then polished them. When I offered a lift to a very senior officer, who told Craven we were a little late, he replied: 'Very well, sir – fasten your belt.' The look on both of their faces I shall never forget. And then there was the occasion when my then adjutant, Captain Jack Boroman was horrified to see Craven on his road bike riding blindingly flat out around and across our assault course to 'tone up his reactions'.

In one of his early appearances for the Aces at New Cross on 29 April 1953, his all-action style of racing brought him into contact with the safety fence. He had scored two second places when he crashed and sustained concussion. But his determination to become a top speedway rider was illustrated by not only his efforts on the track, but also his dedication to the sport by taking what time he could from his army post to ride for the Aces.

George White, another small racer who was a legend at Swindon and a team-mate of Craven's in the England team, recalled the first time he met him at Belle Vue and was struck by how tiny he was.

I first met Peter when he was in the army – I think it was in 1953. I was a junior at the time and I was trying to make my way in the sport. I was in the changing room when Peter came in wearing his army uniform. He was a small chap and he was slim with it. He took off his tunic and his undershirt, which was like a T-shirt, the sleeves were way down to his elbows and the underwear he had on was down to his knees! Although I didn't laugh out loud, I thought it was quite amusing at the time.

In spite of his commitments to the 42nd Lancashire Infantry Division, he found that he had more opportunities to ride for the Aces than ever before. He was becoming a very popular rider with the Hyde Road fans, and he was establishing himself as a valuable reserve that was filling the role of a second string. In fact he was becoming one of the bright spots in an otherwise disappointing season for the Aces. During a league encounter at home to Wimbledon, Craven scored his first paid maximum on 3 October 1953 – a performance that not only confirmed his undoubted talent, but also represented a high point in his season. He had combined with Ken Sharples to reel off three 5-1 heat successes in their 53-31 defeat of the Dons. He had made such an impact during the 1953 season, that he was one of the featured riders in *Speedway Star's* 'Back Cover Boy' series. This was cover dated 10 October 1953, and was obviously printed before the above performance against Wimbledon, but went on to describe him as 'Belle Vue's big bet for stardom' and marvelled at his ability:

Where he gets the strength from to wrestle with that bike of his we'll never know. Somehow he does. And it's right pretty to watch. One day, probably soon, the name Peter Craven will mean maximums for the Manchester team.

Peter finished with his best average yet of 5.83 – 7.71 for just league matches – and was pencilled in for his first full season with the Aces in 1954. He paid tribute to his commanding officer and the club in a column in *Speedway Star*.

I for one thought that speedway would be out for a couple of years, he admitted. *But I counted without a very sympathetic CO. He's been letting me off so that during the past season I've been able to ride in most of my official matches. Another thank you here for Belle Vue, who have been looking after my machine all season. It certainly has been a great relief to me to know that my bike would be in tip-top condition for every meeting.*

Further down his column, he reveals that his lack of height does have some disadvantages when he rides, but his humour is clearly visible:

People ask me what kind of track I like. Well, naturally, the slick ones. Why? Because the rough ones throw me about too much. It's all right for these heavy-weights, but us flea weights; we need 'em smooth. But don't for one minute think that I am trying to put on any weight. No, sir. I'm quite content with my ration and I'm not going in for any of these new fangled courses to put on weight and height. What nature cannot do, I do not propose doing for her.

In the final analysis, Belle Vue avoided the cellar position in the league by just one match point. The season ended on a low note for the Aces when Louis Lawson crashed and fractured his skull – it was an injury that would eventually bring down the flag on his career.

In 1954 food rationing had come to an end following its introduction during the Second World War. Consequently, the mood of the nation was more optimistic than it had been for some time. But speedway racing was suffering, however, because of the increased competition from television and the Entertainments Tax was beginning to take its toll on the sport's dwindling coffers.

Johnnie Hoskins had taken over the promotional reins at Belle Vue in 1953, but Jack Parker remained to lead the side as their captain. He was past his best by now and young riders like Craven and Dick Fisher were emerging to take over from the older riders. Peter Williams also began making a tentative comeback, but it took him a long time to regain his confidence.

Hoskins was a legend in speedway racing, and had already successfully promoted at Wembley and West Ham. It was while he was at West Ham that the burning of his hat became a part of his repertoire. As part of the show Hoskins' would often encourage the riders to get their bikes out on the track with a yell of encouragement and a whack from his hat. In revenge, his team would grab his hat and douse it in methanol and set it alight! This became a regular piece of entertainment, and speedway has never seen his like again. He certainly knew how to promote a speedway event.

He kept the family atmosphere going at Belle Vue, Brenda recalled. *He was a lovely man. His wife was there and Lionel too. They were good times, and of course he used to burn his hat, and Ron Johnston nearly always ended up with it.*

The first meeting of the new season was a challenge match at Swindon which the Robins won 46-37. PC scored 6 points in that encounter, but nine days later in an RAC Cup match at home to Harringay he scorched to a 12-point maximum as the Aces defeated the Racers, 49-35. This was 19 April and he had scored his first full maximum. Although he wasn't consistently hitting big scores, he was easily holding down a heat leader role. Suddenly, Craven had developed from a promising middle-order rider to one of the club's leading riders. His improvement was underlined when he scored his first official full maximum in a league encounter against West Ham on 8 May at Hyde Road – although his performance couldn't prevent the Aces losing to the Hammers 47-37. A week later, on his way to 12 points, he established a new track record of 70.4 seconds at Belle Vue as they defeated Bradford 50-34 in another RAC Cup match.

Once again Belle Vue was experiencing a troubled season as they fought to avoid the wooden spoon just as they did twelve months earlier. Sadly Parker's form was a shadow of what it had been, and by mid-season the experienced veteran was 'rested' and replaced by Don Cuppleditch. But there was still much to learn from the experienced rider and, as Williams recalled, Craven absorbed as much information as he could.

My first memory of Peter was in the Belle Vue dressing room with Jack Parker. It was just the two of us at the end of meeting, and Jack was shaking his head and saying: 'I can't understand the sense in winning a race by 30 yards.' The crowds at that time were huge and Jack would only do enough to win the race. The great attraction at the time for the fans was that Jack would just do enough to win the race by passing his opponent on the run-in from the last bend. The fans, me included, would get so wound up, and Jack would usually win on the line. It was almost as though Jack had saved a little bit of power for the last few yards. To watch Jack Parker holding court as he did after each meeting, standing at the BV starting gate, having his picture taken, signing autographs and not leaving until all were satisfied, he would say to them: 'Have you all done? Can I go now?' Again I think Peter learned from Jack. Your attitude towards your fans is all important, and Peter made himself available to his fans.

Leon Leat also remembered that Peter always had time for his many supporters.

After we loaded up the car, and in those days we used to take the front wheel out and sit the bike on forks on the back of the vehicle, he would sign autographs for the fans and talk to them. He wasn't like some of them are today who sign about three and then walk off, he would sign everyone's. Because of this he was so popular and liked by everyone, and he was often one the last people to leave the stadium.

His former army buddies made arrangements to see their racing soldier in action at Hyde Road. The Mess Secretary organised an outing to watch him at his glorious best, and it was a sight that Lt-Col. Hole never forgot.

It's probably my most vivid memory I have of this pocket-sized sportsmen, he wrote. *Peter ensured that we were specially and comfortably seated to watch a spectacle that gave us immense pleasure. He was so small – just over 5 foot – and light that he rarely got away at the start of the race without giving away several yards lead to his heavier competitors. Then by sheer skill and guts he would catch them up on the straights and pass them on the bends, quite often on the outside and winning in times that were invariably the fastest of the meeting.*

Such was his popularity that, when Belle Vue won the match, the applause was not for the team, but a chant of P-E-T-E-R, then a mighty roar of 'Peter Craven'. These tremendous ovations and the adulation of thousands of his teenage followers affected Peter Craven not in the slightest.

Although this letter was passed on to the Craven family following his death and is dated as 1963, the above description could have been taken from any part of his career with the Aces from 1953 onwards. He has been described as the 'darling of the Belle Vue supporters,' and his popularity never wavered throughout his career with the club. Indeed his reputation grew beyond the confines of Belle Vue to national admiration that established him as one of the most popular British riders of all time.

Nicknames are something that have always been a part of human society, and sport is no different. In speedway racing there have been some memorable phrases and nicknames, such as Ken 'the White Ghost' Le Breton, Brian 'Nipper' Crutcher, Lloyd 'Sprouts' Elder, and lately there has been 'Sudden' Sam Ermolenko, Billy 'the Bullet' Hamill and Joe Screen – 'the Screen Machine'. It was inevitable that a combination of Peter's exciting riding style and his tiny cheeky frame would get supporters' imagination working overtime to devise a suitable name for this likeable racer.

During his early days he was known as 'The Imp', which was probably due to his lack of height more than his riding ability. But as he began to take on, and beat, the world's best speedway riders of his era, somewhere along the line he was dubbed 'The Mighty Atom'. No doubt this was because of the explosive way he would storm around the outside of his opponents in breathtaking style. Later of course he was dubbed 'The Wizard of Balance', which aptly described his style of racing. To his many friends he was simply known as 'PC'. It is unusual that one rider would be given so many different monikers, and it is an acknowledgment of his talent and character that he wore them all so well.

As Belle Vue struggled, Craven found that the team began to rely on his performances to contain the opposition. If there was any pressure on him to produce the goods, he didn't show it as he went about scoring points in his usual spectacular style. Although he was still inexperienced, he rose to the challenge and was regularly supporting the Aces' top rider from New Zealand, Ron Johnston, and Ken Sharples.

At one stage the team had won just one of their first eight league matches. But perhaps the lowest point of all was the embarrassing thrashing they received at Wembley. For years the Wembley Lions and Belle Vue battled for the honour to be the sport's most glamorous club; so to be crushed 67-17 left the Aces' faces as red as their race-jackets – not one rider scored more than 4 points! In the return they fared little better, losing 46-37. But the Lions really rubbed their noses in it when they came back to Hyde Road and won 59-29 – this was not a good year to be an Aces' supporter.

Nonetheless, Craven continued to shine with an 18-point maximum in their 71-37 victory over Poole in a National Trophy match, and he was regularly finishing the matches in double figures. Such was his progress, that to watch him race now it was hard to believe that he was the same rider that Liverpool had released on a free transfer. Moreover, the best was yet to come. At the other end of the scale, Parker's performances were giving cause for concern. But Williams believed that it was the youthful zest of riders like Craven and Dick Fisher that ushered in a new era.

As men we were really only young lads. When Peter got going it really sig-nalled the end for the older riders. Some had been racing pre-war, but they had their lives spoilt by the war. After the war years I would think a lot of young men were influenced into a life as a speedway rider by watching Peter. He was completely without malice or bad thoughts or habits. There would only be a few years between us all, but some of us would get distracted by the fans – but not Peter. He was to me, honest and straight. He was a lovely lad, who developed into a lovely man. His brother, Brian, was very like him. I don't think he ever changed or got spoilt. I don't think I ever met his mother and father, but they would be of my parent's generation and they expected you to behave properly.

Injuries are an occupational hazard in speedway racing, but a rider doesn't expect to be the victim of a rider-less bike. However, as Frank Maclean reported, that's what very nearly happened to Peter during a second-half race at Belle Vue when he was locked in a struggle with team-mates Ron Johnston and Ken Sharples. Sharples, who was trail-ing in third, suddenly hit trouble on the third lap when his throttle jammed open – there were no cut-out cables in those days. But when he attempted to lay down his machine, to his amazement his bike corrected itself and took off without him!

We watched in horror as the machine mounted the grass verge and roared across the centre green towards the starting area, wrote Maclean. *Meanwhile Craven and Johnston were racing in a terrific duel around the pits bend and heading towards the finish line in one direction as the rider-less bike veered towards them from the other. The two Belle Vue stars reached the line together as Sharples' machine, twisting and turning, thankfully crashed into the safety fence just in front of them.*

Almost without question, it is every rider's dream to be World Speedway Champion – and Peter Craven was no different. Indeed, he had already expressed his desire to become the world's best rider while he was working with Charlie Oates. Therefore he entered the World title hunt for the first time.

In those days the World Championship qualification system saw the British and Commonwealth riders compete in a series of qualifying rounds on British tracks. The best from the Second Division then joined the best from the First Division in two qualifying meetings to determine the sixteen riders for the final. They would be drawn to ride at two different tracks, and the top sixteen scorers would then qualify for the World Championship Final at Wembley.

Peter entered the World Championship chase for the first time at Hyde Road on 14 August 1954. Among the sixteen-man line-up for this qualifying round were some of his team-mates, Sharples, Johnston and Harry Edwards, two Swedes, Kjell Carlsson and the charismatic Olle Nygren, and the defending World Champion, Freddie Williams. But from his very first race it was clear that Peter meant business when he recovered from a 'full locker' to battle his way past Dick Bradley and then Edwards, while Scotsman Ken McKinley crashed out, and he had begun his World Championship campaign with a victory. In front of a capacity crowd he won the meeting with an impressive 15-point maximum, and *Speedway Star* said that he was 'at least 40 yards in front at the tapes'.

Four days later he was in action at Harringay for his second round. Split Waterman may have taken the top spot with a 14-point score, but all the attention centred on The Mighty Atom who became the first rider to make sure of his place in the World Final by finishing second with 13 points. He dropped his only points to Waterman and to Jim Lightfoot – who was a shock winner as he came in as a replacement for the injured Ron How.

The little Liverpudlian had qualified for his first World Individual Championship final. He was Belle Vue's only World Finalist that year, and he qualified with a total of 28 points and finished the qualifiers in joint second place with Eddie Rigg – former World Champion Jack Young led the field with 29 points.

Craven had more or less established himself as the Aces' number one rider, and his form earned him his first call-up to ride for England in the three-match Test series against Australasia – this was a formidable team that was made up of the best from Australia and New Zealand. He made his debut at reserve in the opening Test at West Ham on 10 August 1954, which the hosts won 60-48. He appeared in heat 15 with Freddie Williams, but crashed out as the Australasian pairing of Geoff Mardon and Jack Biggs scored a 5-1 heat win. The Second Test match was staged at Belle Vue, and this time Peter scored 7 points as England took another 64-44 victory to clinch the series with one Test remaining at Bradford. The English team completed a white-wash over the Australasian side with a 56-52 win, but Peter scored just 1 point at the Yorkshire circuit.

Peter was a modest rider and believed that everyone should be given their chance to shine on merit. He caused a sensation one year when he turned down an opportunity to ride for England because he felt that his form wasn't good enough. Some reports say that this was a Test match at Bradford in 1954, but I believe that it was the following year in 1955. According to the *Speedway Star Digest 1962*, Peter scored 1 point for England at Bradford in '54, but he didn't appear in the corresponding fixture the following year. Therefore, I am quite certain that it was in 1955, especially when you see that he scored 15 points in a later meeting in the series.

Nonetheless Peter warmed up for the World Championship by winning a best pairs competition with Dick Fisher at Belle Vue. As a pair they scored 17 points with Peter securing 14 of the duo's total.

Just over a year since joining Belle Vue, he had qualified for his first World Final, established himself as the club's top rider, and become an England international. It was of little wonder that the Manchester faithful had taken the spectacular rider to their hearts, and he felt that he had a real chance of doing well in his first World Final.

Three

ALL ROADS LEAD TO WEMBLEY

The Empire Stadium, Wembley is arguably the most famous sporting stadium in the world. These days it is synonymous with football and the FA Cup and, of course, that historic day in 1966 when Bobby Moore led the nation's football heroes to World Cup success. However, when the stadium was pulled down for redevelopment in 2002, the historians who mulled over the debris of its rich and colourful past hardly mentioned that it was the spiritual home of speedway racing.

Johnnie Hoskins, the man who is credited with starting the sport way back in 1923 in West Maitland, Australia, received a well-timed telephone call from his friend, Lionel Wills, who suggested that he should get in touch with the stadium owner at that time, Arthur Elvin. It seemed that Elvin was looking for a manager as he intended to stage speedway racing inside the stadium. After an encouraging meeting, the Wembley Lions speedway team was born.

The Lions took to the track for the first time on 16 May 1929, and Hoskins' brief was simply to create a championship-winning team. He duly obliged by putting together a side that won successive titles in 1930, 1931, and 1932. Along with Belle Vue, they were one of the teams to beat, and in the immediate post-war years they were even more successful with seven league titles to their name until they closed after the 1956 season. Under Elvin, no one presented speedway racing with the same degree of style and flamboyance. The Lions returned for a brief two-year spell during the early 1970s, but they couldn't recapture the glory years.

Brian Crutcher was riding for Wembley in 1954, and he recalled that speedway racing was still attracting healthy audiences despite predictions of doom and gloom.

Speedway in the Fifties was good – it was tremendous. At Wembley we used to get crowds of 45-50,000 people and on World Final night the place was packed with nearly 90,000 people in the stadium. Down here at Poole they still get decent crowds, but those sort of crowds for a league match are unheard of now.

Nonetheless, it wasn't league racing that made the stadium so special for speedway fans; it was the sport's premier event – the World Individual Championship Final. It was staged for the first time in 1936, and except for the war, it remained at Wembley until 1961 when Sweden became the first country outside of Britain to stage the Final – Wembley then shared the event on a rotation basis with firstly Sweden, and then Poland. Other tournaments were also held at the stadium that included Test matches, World Championship qualifying rounds, and the World Team Cup; but it was the World Final that created that celebrated 'Magic of Wembley'. World Final night was a spell-binding experience; once savoured, it was never forgotten.

I witnessed the last World Final to be staged at the twin towers in 1981, when the American Bruce Penhall won the first of his two World titles in one of the best Wembley finals ever staged. The atmosphere was incredible, the roar of the crowd reduced the noise of the engines to a mere hum, and yet that hum was the amplifier for all of the excitement that was felt by the thousands crammed inside the stadium. This wasn't ear-splitting volume of the kind you will experience inside Cardiff's Millennium Stadium where the British Speedway Grand Prix is now held, but a comforting, all-enveloping cushion of speed and exhilaration.

From a riders' point of view it was a different experience. This big old stadium could be a terrifying prospect when it was packed with around 90,000 speedway supporters, all cheering their heroes and jeering their villains. Sweden's Ove Fundin admitted that he found the place 'frightening and intimidating', when he qualified for his debut World Final in 1954. It was a place where speedway dreams were realised, and speedway hearts were broken.

The atmosphere of a World Final at Wembley was electric, agreed Leon Leat. *It was a one-off night and the excitement of it was incredible. You just couldn't recreate it anywhere else, and anything could happen. The track wasn't very good, though, and Peter always said that they should have the Final at Belle Vue's Hyde Road because it was such a brilliant track.*

Reigning champion Freddie Williams of Wales was a shock casualty of the qualifying rounds, as he failed to make the cut and had to be content with a reserve spot for the 1954 final. He had won the title twice, and this was the first indication that a new era of speedway riders were about to wrestle glory away from the grasp of the post-war stars. As Williams sat in the pits, 80,000 people were watching a unique encounter taking place on the track between the old stars and the new stars. This World Final was the first of the post-war finals that was not a sell out, and it was another indication that the 'boom period' for British speedway was coming to an end.

England's first World Champion, Tommy Price, the legendary Split Waterman, Fred Brand and Eddie Rigg would not appear in a Wembley Final again. Australian, Jack Young – who was the first and, so far, only Second Division rider to win the World title – along with Price and the inactive Williams, had shared the championship since 1949. There were three riders who made their debut that evening, who would emerge from this night of learning to become a trio of the very best: Barry Briggs, Peter Craven and Ove Fundin.

The Final was considered to be one of the most open for years, with the experts predicting that a winner would come from any of the following riders: Young, Brian Crutcher, Olle Nygren, Waterman, Rigg, Arthur Forrest, or the wonder kid from New Zealand, Ronnie Moore. Moore was riding just ten weeks after he had broken his left leg, and with the aid of a special brace he took his place in the meeting – some critics wrote off his chances because of the injury.

In the long history of the World Final, very few riders have won the title in their debut appearance in the sport's blue riband event. Freddie Williams in 1950, and Gary Havelock in 1992, are the real debut victors, as Lionel Van Praag's win during the first staging in 1936 doesn't really count as all sixteen competitors were debutants that night. Furthermore, Aussie Van Praag had already appeared in the 1935 Star Championship – which was the forerunner to the World Championship – so it is appropriate to say that there have only ever really been two debut winners. Therefore, a night of glory was very much stacked against World Final virgins.

Not many people gave Craven a hope of making much of an impression, except Birmingham skipper Alan Hunt, who was quoted in *Speedway News* as saying that Craven and Eddie Rigg may have a battle for third place, but believed that Jack Young was the likely winner. Naturally there was no shortage of optimism coming from the Manchester area, which led to the *Speedway Gazette* journalist R.M. Samuel suggesting that a reader from Belle Vue was slightly misguided in her prediction that PC would win the title. He based his opinion on having seen the Aces struggle so much throughout the season.

Craven was wearing the number nine race-jacket for his first 'big night' which meant that he appeared in heats 3 and 5, and would then have a long gap of five races before he would appear again in heat 11. The best thing about the draw was that in his last two races he would start from the inside berths.

The significance of heats 18 and 19 would not emerge for another twelve months. It was as if the speedway gods had decreed that it was time that the old master Price finally moved away from the throne room, and made way for a brave new prince.

There is definitely something to be said for the old adage: 'If at first you don't succeed, try, try again,' and it is one that certainly fits the career of 'The Mighty Atom'. His first World Final appearance did not exactly get the sport's journalists scurrying off to tell the nation that a new star had emerged. Indeed, all the talk was of the brave performance of Moore and the silver medal for Brian Crutcher – a performance that had most experts writing his name down as a future champion.

Peter appeared in heat 3 against former champion Jack Young, and the Swedish duo of Olle Nygren, and Ove Fundin. He fell off and failed to score. Only a slight improvement followed in his second race when he managed to complete four laps, but still trailed in last behind fellow countrymen Rigg, Trevor Redmond and the renowned 'Black Prince' Arthur Forrest. In heat 11 he was fourth again, this time behind eventual champion Moore, Tommy Price and Geoff Mardon. At the interval stage, Craven was bottom of the list with no points, and the southerners in the stadium must have wondered just what Belle Vue were getting so excited about. This was especially so when he finished fourth again behind his fellow countrymen Crutcher, Fred Brand and Split Waterman.

Then he lined-up in his final race facing Barry Briggs, Jack Biggs and Aub Lawson. Heat 18 saw him finally make a decent start and he emerged from a first bend scramble as the leader, and stormed away for his first win. He received a hero's welcome when he returned to the pits. This victory meant that he would not finish in last place overall; that dubious distinction went to none other than Sweden's Ove Fundin.

It hadn't been a good final for me. I had scored 2 points, and I thought, well at least I won't finish last, said Fundin. *Then this little fella from England, Peter Craven, who hadn't scored a point all night, won his last race and I was last after all! So I had to take some consolation from the fact that I was among the top sixteen riders in the world, which for a person like me, from the back-waters of Sweden, was a big achievement.*

New Zealand's wonder boy, Ronnie Moore, whose title aspirations appeared to be in tatters earlier in the season when he broke his leg, defied all the odds to win his first World title with a 15-point maximum. Furthermore he was the youngest-ever winner at that time. Second place went to Crutcher with 13 points and he defeated Sweden's Olle Nygren for the silver medal position in a run-off. A new generation of world beaters had emerged, and Peter Craven had a hand on their coat tails.

It is remarkable that he had such an effective season when you consider that he achieved all this while he was still seeing out his national service. When the season came to an end, Belle Vue had managed to avoid the bottom of the league by the narrowest of margins during the club's final match of the season at Birmingham.

This match proved to be Jack Parker's final match for the team, and it was an encounter that the club had to win to avoid the wooden spoon for the first time in the club's history. Birmingham, who had experienced a troubled season, had also been struggling near the foot of the league table, and this was most definitely a battle for pride.

Despite a first race fall, Parker's experience came to the fore when he combined with Ron Johnston to secure an important 5-1 score in the twelfth race that all but clinched a vital win. Belle Vue eventually won the match 44-38 – Peter scored 7 points – and it was a victory that ensured that they evaded the cellar position and their reputation remained intact.

Johnnie Hoskins was a real showman, a man who knew how to promote a speedway event, and he was also always good for a quote. Following his team's success at Birmingham, while referring to the handing over of the wooden spoon to the Brummies, he was quoted as saying: 'Nobody can accuse us of not giving anything away.'

The retirement of Parker indicated the beginning of a new era for Belle Vue Speedway. The team for 1955 was built around the emerging talent of Craven, Johnston and Fisher. But the big news at the close of season was that Split Waterman was scheduled to ride for the Aces. Waterman had a reputation as a bit of a clown off the track, but there was no denying his ability onboard a speedway machine. He had forged a worthy reputation riding for clubs in the capital, and had made five World Final appearances – his best performance was a runners-up place in the 1953 final.

Following the closure of Harringay, Waterman – along with the rest of the team – was placed at the mercy of the Speedway Control Board who would decide where the riders would be placed. Immediately he was linked with Wimbledon as Ronnie Moore had indicated that he wouldn't be returning to race in Britain. However, the new World Champion had a change of heart, and Split was then linked with the Aces. But this fell through and he eventually joined West Ham.

None of this bothered Peter Craven as he prepared for the 1955 season, as his confidence was given a boost by the knowledge that he would be free from any restrictions that national service had previously placed upon him. He was expected to make significant progress that year, and as the season commenced with a series of open meetings and challenge matches, no one could have known just what the year would have in store for the lad from Liverpool.

There were just seven teams competing in the First Division in 1955 and for a rider like Craven who had yet to really establish himself at international level, he had to work in between his racing engagements in order to not only make a living, but also to maintain his equipment. When he left the army he joined his brother Brian and worked for Langham Engineering, which was situated in the Everton Valley.

Belle Vue began the new campaign by setting the pace at the top of the league. Sharples, Johnston and Craven formed a formidable heat leader trio, but they were receiving some solid support from Bob Duckworth, Harry Edwards, Don Cuppleditch, Fisher and Peter Williams. Brian Craven also appeared for the Aces' second team as well as riding in second halves at the Zoo. A narrow 2-point victory over Wimbledon – who included Moore and Barry Briggs in their team – suggested that they were not going to struggle through the season like they had done in 1954. Peter Williams was particularly happy with the way that Ken Sharples would approach his role as the captain.

I always felt that we were very lucky young riders at Belle Vue to have him as captain, said Williams. *I thought he was the best in the country, though Bradford riders will say that Ron Clarke was a great captain – I liked them both.*

Despite their promising start, there were some sections of the sport's press that was expecting Peter to cut loose straightaway and score heavily. In late April *Speedway Star* carried a photo of 'The Wizard of Balance' and its caption said that there were some Aces' supporters who had expected a larger points return from him. It was true that a bundle of double figures had yet to come his way, but by June he had sneaked into the league's top ten scorers.

Nonetheless he produced an impressive display in the club's 49-47 win at Norwich when he scored 14 points, and this performance represented a turn in fortunes for that year. He finished with 11 points in the Astorias Trophy at Belle Vue that was won by skipper Sharples. His 11 points put him in joint fourth. The pleasing aspect about it was that field included Briggs, Moore, Tommy Price and Eric Williams, who were all riding well that year. Incidentally, finishing at the bottom of the pack with 3 points was Brian Craven, who was drafted in as a replacement for Ronnie Moore who had to withdraw after the early stages of the meeting because of mechanical gremlins.

Peter's attentions focused on the World Championship on 13 August, when he travelled to Birmingham for the first of his two qualifying rounds. The meeting was won by South African Doug Davies with a perfect 15-point maximum, with Peter finishing runner-up with 14 points – dropping his only point to Davies. His second and final qualifying round was at Belle Vue.

Having already scored 14 points, it seemed that qualification on his home track was a mere formality, and he didn't disappoint – he won the meeting with a 15-point maximum and made sure of his place in the final. However, in his final race, he called upon all of his skills to see off a determined challenge from Split Waterman. Waterman made life difficult for him on the first bend, and the report in the *Speedway Gazette* indicated that he nearly fell off as a result of a squeeze that the experienced Waterman had put on the Belle Vue Ace. But Peter's talents were an equal to these tactics, and he took control and roared away to victory. This was another indication that the old guard were moving over to make way for the new generation of British riders coming up through the ranks.

Once again Craven had finished the qualifying rounds with 29 points, and was in joint first place with Jack Young. With one World Final appearance already under his belt, he was hopeful of making a better impression than the one he made on his debut. Defending champion Ronnie Moore had qualified along with his Wimbledon team-mate Barry Briggs. Craven was joined by his team-mate from Belle Vue, Ron Johnston, who also made his first Final with 26 points.

But this was the first time that the top four qualifiers from the Continental Final qualified directly to Wembley. Ove Fundin had qualified along with fellow countrymen Olle Nygren, and Kjell Carlsson, while the final place was taken by Henry Anderson.

As the build-up began for the big night at Wembley, *Speedway Gazette* contributor, Colin Warren, thought that Peter was a dark horse for the championship, but added that he never performed very well at Wembley. This was underlined when the Aces lost a National Trophy match at the Empire Stadium earlier in the season, and PC scored just 5 points. If it was held at Hyde Road he would have been a red-hot favourite to win, a fact that was illustrated to good effect a week or so before the Final when he scorched to a 15-point maximum as the Aces defeated West Ham 62-34. The *Speedway Star* correspondent enthused that he had 'never been on better form,' and he had swept around the outside of Hammers' duo Jack Biggs and Waterman as if they were 'standing still'.

In spite of this impressive performance his chances were virtually written off by most of the so-called experts in their previews. *Speedway Star's* Danny Carter admitted that he would like to see him do well, but believed that his inconsistent gating would let him down. Further on in their preview issue another scribe acknowledged that unless he could trap, he would not be a factor. As far as the informed pundits were concerned, Brian Crutcher on his home circuit was England's best hope of glory. Defending title holder Ronnie Moore and his Wimbledon colleague, Barry Briggs were thought to have a good chance, as was Olle Nygren. Everyone but a few wrote off Peter's chances on two grounds: he wasn't a consistently good starter, and he hadn't performed particularly well at Wembley.

The great thing about Peter Craven as a speedway rider was that he would often score his points by passing riders from the back. It is an unfortunate fact that to be successful in World Championship speed-way racing, the rider cannot rely alone on his ability to be able to come from behind. Such is the quality of riders in a World Championship that once they are in front, they are difficult to pass. The sport has a history of very spectacular and exciting riders who are adept at passing but that have never won the World title.

Peter Williams offered this view on his style and ability:

I have already said that the leg trailers were much more of a 'balancing' type of rider than the foot forward rider. I don't think Peter was so exceptional at the time – Billy Bales was almost identical. The real image of Peter was that he never gave up. He was not always the best of starters, but he would work his body over the bike to win. It was his way of lying off his bike to get maximum drive that made him so popular. He was never boastful, and I think that is why he is so well thought of by those of us who are still living.

The 1955 World Final was covered by the BBC, and what a Final it turned out to be for the world's most famous broadcasting corporation. The commentator was Dennis Monger, while 1949 World Champion Tommy Price was on hand to provide his 'advisory comments'.

Among the 54,000-strong crowd at Wembley on 15 September were members of Peter's family.

We always had seats in the stadium, Brenda recalled. *I would always sit with Mr Craven, while Brian and Joan had seats as well. It was a marvellous occasion. You could sit there and look round the packed stadium and see all the club colours scattered around the stands. It was very colourful and exciting.*

The *Speedway Gazette* conducted quite an in-depth description of the final, and it claimed that they had adopted a system of reporting that had never been done before. They carried out a heat-by-heat report of the meeting by beginning in the press gallery, then the story moved to the Royal Box, then into the pits, and onto the centre green where their cameraman, Les Clayton, was situated. They also used material from one of their journalists who was watching from the back straight, and went by the name of Pegasus. He was among some of the passionate Belle Vue supporters. Whether it worked or not is a matter of opinion, but what it does achieve is to offer some interesting insights into one of the most memorable finals in the history of the competition.

This time Peter was drawn at number eight for the final. His first race was in heat 2, and he sped to victory in the fastest time of the night as he defeated Fundin, Johnston and Nygren. It was reported that he hardly put his foot down as he stormed around the 344-metre (378 yards) track in breathtaking style. Just to confound his critics, he produced a start that the *Speedway Gazette* described as a 'flier'. Riding an engine prepared by Harold Jackson and tuned by Wilf Lucy, he emerged for his second race and made light work of defeating Arthur Forrest, Eric Williams and Henry Andersen. But then he dropped his first point of the evening to Briggs in heat 11, despite pressing him for the lead early on. After all the riders had completed three rides, it was Peter and Briggs who led the field with 8 points each, and they were followed by defending champion Moore and Crutcher with 7 points.

'I didn't expect anything like this,' Craven told *Gazette* journalist Fred Philpot when he returned to the pits after his Titanic battle with Briggs. 'The only trouble now is that I am going so well, I shall be disappointed if I start falling away.'

Significantly, PC was sat next to Fundin in the pits, when the Swede admitted to them that his nerves had played a big part in his disappointing score of 4 points from three starts. In a gesture that was typical of Craven's character, he tried to put the Swede at his ease with some friendly words of encouragement. Later in his career, of course, Ove Fundin would go on to become one of his biggest rivals. But those words obviously had a calming and positive effect upon him, as he then went out in heat 15 and won his first race in a World Final. Little could Peter have known how those words of encouragement would eventually affect his own fortunes that night – and unwittingly sew the seeds for the beginning of one of speedway's greatest World Final performers.

It was reported that when Peter emerged for his fourth ride in heat 14, there was a steely look of determination on his face as he mounted his machine to face the defending champion, Moore, while both Sweden's Kjell Carlsson and fellow countryman Phil Clarke were merely making up the numbers. Cruicially, Eric Williams had beaten Briggs in the previous heat, so it was a race that was vital to both Craven and Moore's title hopes.

Peter was starting from gate three, while Moore had the inside berth. In a night when everything seemed to be going the Belle Vue rider's way, he emerged from the tight first turn in the lead. He roared around the track to the delight of the cheering crowd, but the Kiwi Moore continued to pressure the young Englishman – one mistake, a lapse in concentration, and he would be through. But there was no denying PC as he swept to a victory that put him 1 point clear of his nearest rival Briggs – with just one round of races to go.

Craven appeared for his final race in heat 17 to face the local hero Brian Crutcher. Critics in the stadium felt that Crutcher's local knowledge of the track as a Wembley rider would surely defeat The Mighty Atom – who up until this night had not exactly got to grips with the Wembley track. Crutcher, who had finished runner-up in 1954, saw his hopes of glory crash when he fell off and was excluded from his fourth ride. This race was an all–English encounter as the other two riders were Billy Bales and Cyril Roger. But if Craven was looking for any favours from his fellow countrymen, he could forget it – this was the World Championship!

From the inside gate it was Crutcher who led into the first bend, while Craven discovered that gate two was not so favourable and he found himself behind Bales in third place. In his characteristic style he fought his way past the Norwich rider and set about pressuring the Lions' favourite, Crutcher. He had the crowd on their feet as he tried everything he could to find a way by; because if he finished in first place then he would clinch the World title. In a pulsating four laps Crutcher resisted the persistent Craven and held on to win the race, while PC finished second with a total of 13 points to his name.

Therefore, Peter would have to wait to see if he had done enough. New Zealand's Barry Briggs had to win heat 20 to tie with him and force a run-off for the 1955 World Championship. The Kiwi faced Sweden's Ove Fundin, Arthur Forrest and Carlsson.

Before the race, *Gazette* journalist Philpot had been speaking to Fundin who said of Craven: 'That's one rider I should like to see take the title. He's a good 'un and such a nice lad too.' As the Swedish rider walked over to his machine to prepare for the final heat, Philpot reported that he informed him that if he defeated Briggs, then PC would be champion. Fundin was said to have responded: 'I ride to win.'

The excitement in the stands of the old stadium was electric as the four riders arrived at the tapes for the final programmed race. In Peter's corner of the pits and among his Aces' supporters, the tension was heart-stopping. There was nothing they could do – it was a case of watch and see.

Fundin took up the inside gate position, while Briggs was alongside in gate two. The patriotic crowd prayed for any victory other than one for the New Zealander. As the tapes rose it was the Swede who hit the front, with Briggs tucked in behind. After one lap had been completed, Fundin remained in the lead despite the efforts of the Kiwi. Briggs was known for his hard, uncompromising style of riding, and while the ice-cool Swede looked to be in control as he emerged from the second bend, everyone inside the stadium knew that Briggs wouldn't give up until the chequered flag had fallen.

Meanwhile, Peter watched intensely from the pit gate. He rode every lap with the Swede, hoping that he would repel the challenge from Briggs. It was reported that in his excitement at what was unfolding before him, the tiny Craven was practically hanging over the pit gate and on the track – which resulted in one of the officials picking him off the gate! Not to be denied, he again excitedly took up his position on the gate as another lap was completed.

Briggs tried everything to find a way past Fundin, but it wasn't to be and the biggest cheer of Fundin's career greeted his race win. Craven celebrated too, and he danced a jig of delight as he had accomplished his dream of becoming World Champion.

Once again the *Gazette* was on hand to capture his immediate reaction to his triumph.

Can I really remember what happened during those 72.6 seconds? Was it really true that Ove Fundin, with whom I had been chatting to only a moment or two ago, went out and beat Barry Briggs, thus leaving me a clear point ahead of three riders who had totalled twelve? I do remember, of course, but as I stood there by the pit gates, hardly bothering about the shale which was thrown up, it seemed unreal that, because Ove had won, I was the new champion. Barry tried terribly hard, and Arthur Forrest was near him all the time, but Fundin was the first man home. I didn't see Forrest and Carlsson cross the line, for many hands grabbed mine to offer their congratulations. I was all mixed up, but I knew I'd won and that, after all, to me, was what mattered most.

England celebrated a new hero, and he was the most popular winner since Bluey Wilkinson's triumph in 1938. His victory was greeted with such cheer and jubilation that another twenty-six years would pass before another rider would sample such public adoration again. Furthermore he was the youngest rider to win the title at that time, beating the previous winner, Ronnie Moore, by a few months; and he was also the first British rider to win the title from outside of London. He had done it and when – with exception of the Manchester faithful – most of the critics had written him off because he couldn't gate, or because he had such a poor record at Wembley. But his talent shone through. With just four years of speedway under his belt he had won the World Championship – Britain had discovered a very bright star that September night who was destined to shine for many years to come.

All I took for my nerves was an aspirin, he revealed. *It helped to keep me awake. I drove all the way down from Liverpool, and yet my reaction tonight seems better than ever.*

He received the *Sunday Dispatch* World Championship trophy from Field Marshal Earl Alexander of Tunis. Moore defeated Briggs in a run-off to finish as the runner-up to Craven, while Briggs had to settle for third place on the podium. No one, it seemed, begrudged the likeable Scouser his moment of glory, even though he was a surprise winner. Former Wembley Lion, Crutcher, recalled:

I beat Peter in my race with him but he wasn't one of the fancied contenders. We all knew he had the ability to win, but he grabbed the opportunity with both hands. It was his night.

It's not unusual for riders to have routines and rituals that they carry out before they begin a night's racing. Some riders wear a lucky t-shirt under their leathers, others insist that no one cleans their helmet and goggles in between races except themselves; and some even believe that it's bad luck if women are present in the pits! After the celebrations of Peter's sensational triumph at Wembley, when he was asked what the secret of his success was by Len Went, editor of the *Speedway News,* he responded: 'I always wear a pair of pyjamas under my leathers. It sort of gives me a comfy feeling. I certainly wouldn't go out on the track without them.'

Furthermore, many years later, another journalist noted that his pyjamas were a shade of purple and white. He believed that it used to be red and white, but as the years had passed the red had faded to a shade of purple. When he enquired why he chose to ride in purple, the quick-witted World Champion replied: 'Because it happens to match Johnnie Hoskins' language when Johnno burns his hat!'

One of the many admirable qualities of Craven's character was how thoughtful he was, and this was highlighted in Barry Briggs' column in *Speedway Star.*

The best story of the night, wrote Briggo, *revolves around the new champion Peter Craven. He was running around with a cheque for £500 in his hand and trying to borrow enough ready cash to send a telegram to his old Army CO, Lt-Col. Hole of the R.A.O.C. to tell of his success.*

There were many people that Peter felt he had to thank, but he told the *Gazette* that it was journalist Frank Maclean whose heart to heart with the little champion brought about a change to his outlook.

I must date my success back to a chat I had with a journalist, Frank Maclean. Frank proved to me that I had great possibilities and capabilities, and that changed my whole outlook. I must thank him indirectly for my surprising success. Already I have had offers to ride in Poland, Austria and one from Ove Fundin to go to Sweden. I shall think them over, but a lot depends on Harold [Jackson] *and Wilf* [Lucy]. *The money I shall put in the bank, it will come in very handy. It's grand to be the first Belle Vue victor and I only hope that I shall prove to be a worthy champion.*

There were very few who didn't doubt that he would be anything other than a worthy champion. Deposed champion Ronnie Moore, also writing in *Speedway Star,* said:

Let me say here and now that with Peter Craven the crown is in good hands. He gave the crowd what they wanted at Wembley: thrills, speed and the unexpected. He was the underdog on the night, and I can't recall anyone tipping him as a stone ginger certainty! But much more than being better than the rest of us for one meeting, Peter has been thrilling the crowds all year with his new style of riding. A style which calls for a wonderful sense of balance, and one which has caused this magazine to call him, 'the nearest thing to Oliver Hart'. Good luck Peter, you said after the title was yours that you hoped to be able to live up to it — you will.

While all the sport's press celebrated a British triumph, journalist Barney Bamford was one of the few who suggested that some caution should be exercised over the surprise result. Writing in *Speedway News,* he acknowledged that he was the best rider on the night, but asked: 'Is Craven a worthy World Champion? Is he in the same category as Jack Young, Ronnie Moore and Barry Briggs? In my opinion he is not!'

Bamford went on to suggest that the formula should be revised, so that the champion is the rider who is the most consistent over a season. He also wrote that as far as he could recall only the 'dumb typist' in the *Speedway News* office had tipped the tiny Craven to win. Perhaps this was another indication of the north and south divide, as Tony Mann recalled:

He was very well thought of up here in the north, but down south they took a while to catch on. Peter used to go to Wembley in the early days and get nought, so they didn't really rate him. But when he won the World Championship that changed all that.

Frank Maclean was one of the first to receive a visit of thanks from Peter when he returned to Liverpool, as he revealed in his article in *Speedway News.*

It seemed typical of Peter that having driven back through the night from Wembley to his home town Liverpool that he should want to thank the people who, so he said, helped him on the way to Wembley. That was Peter's reason for him coming to my flat with his charming girlfriend Brenda and putting the World trophy on my sideboard.

In Maclean's article Peter also expressed his thanks to the supporters:

At Wembley they were grand, and at Belle Vue the Aces' fans have helped no end. Don't believe those people who think that cheers and enthusiasm are lost in the roars of the motors. It's more about what you feel in the atmosphere than the actual noise and it makes no end of difference.

Peter embarked on a tour of gratitude that included everyone who had helped him during his four years as a speedway racer.

I remember going to Wembley with Bob Duckworth and shouting myself hoarse along with 54,000 others, Peter Williams recollected. *I didn't know I had lost my voice until I couldn't speak the next morning. I was working at the shop with my young brother, when about 5.30 in the afternoon, Peter pulled up in his Jowett Jupiter. On the passenger seat was this huge cup. He had called in especially to show it to us. To me first and then Wilf Lucy, who was the engine man at BV and he was around the corner, so then he went round there to show Wilf. That's just an example of how thoughtful he was to others.*

Charlie Oates also recalled another thoughtful gesture from Peter and it is a memory that he treasures to this day. 'When he won the title in 1955, he brought the trophy to work and put it on my desk and said: "I won it for you." That was a proud moment; and I often shed a little tear when I think of him. We were very close.'

There were others that he called upon to express his gratitude, including Eric Langton, Alice Hart, Harold Jackson and Harry Welch, and he also fitted in an interview with Alan Clarke at the BBC Studios in Manchester that evening. By the time he had arrived at Belle Vue to ride, he was beginning to feel tired from all the excitement. Not that it seemed to show in his first race as he battled his way from the back to beat his team-mate, Dick Fisher, by inches on the line. He dropped just 1 point during the qualifying rounds in the hastily arranged Supporters' Trophy. But after qualifying for the winner-takes-all Grand Final, he finished third behind Ron Johnston and Ken Sharples – perhaps by then the emotional rollercoaster that he had experienced over the last twenty-four hours was slowing down, and fatigue was settling in.

He received a hero's welcome at Belle Vue, and all of his family, friends and supporters were very proud indeed of their talented young rider.

He received a wonderful reception from the public and there was a special pres-entation made by the starting gate, and we were all very proud of him. The family had a photograph taken together with Peter and the trophy at Belle Vue. It was one of the rare occasions when Peter's mother attended a speedway meeting, revealed Brenda. *It wasn't that through a lack on interest, as she followed Peter and Brian's careers avidly and put together a much treasured album of their career. She was very proud of the success Peter had, it was simply because she was fearful and couldn't bear to watch. Peter thought the world of his mother – as well as his father – and she was a good, caring person. I well remember the times during the early days when we used to come back from Ainsdale, freezing cold and soaking wet; and she always had a warm fire waiting for us and a big roast dinner. They were happy times.*

One of his first overseas engagements as the World Champion was a trip to Sweden and Norway. He travelled with the Belle Vue team manager, Harold Jackson, to the airport in London, and he was grateful for his navigational knowledge as they drove through thick fog to get to the capital. However, on arriving at the airport they found that they were without the necessary flight cards that they needed to be able to board a flight to Sweden. Unfortunately, because of their lack of experience in foreign travel, they had little knowledge of how to go about resolving the problem. Luckily Split Waterman came to their rescue and they were able to climb aboard their aircraft. Swedish representative Charles Ringblom met them at the airport and they were taken to their hotel.

The next day Peter borrowed a Rover car from Ringblom and proceeded to take in the sights. However, as he revealed in his column in *Speedway News*, he didn't get to see as much as he would have liked because of the local drivers.

The stop-start driving had me guessing at first, then when I got the idea I just drifted into being just another menace and began to enjoy it. What a sensation – almost as good as the 'Bobs' at Belle Vue!

Peter appeared in front of 20,000 fans and raced in an individual meeting at Gothenburg. The Swedes were a fast-emerging speedway nation, with stars like Fundin and Nygren in particular putting the Scandinavian country on the speedway map. The meeting was won by

Barry Briggs with a 15-point maximum, but Peter's lack of experience in Sweden was too much of a handicap to seriously challenge for a rostrum finish.

'I knew the Swedish boys had defeated Australasia 2-1, and of course they must be good to be able to do that,' said Craven in an interview that appeared in the *Speedway Gazette*. 'But I got a shock when looking at Rune Sormander in the first heat at Gothenburg. He never gave Ronnie Moore the slightest possibility to follow him and I started to think it over.'

He was third in his first race behind Briggs and Phil Clark, and he was caught out by the slippery conditions in his next race and finished in fourth. But by heat 9, he had decided that it was now or never to make his mark on the meeting.

I felt better when I made the gate and left Neil Street and Split Waterman behind me. The two remaining heats gave me a further 6 points and I started to know the track and how to gate. But then it was too late!

Peter finished with 10 points and was joint fourth with Sormander and Moore. But he was impressed by the quality of riders that Sweden could field and, no doubt sensing the potential of the Scandinavians, he suggested that a Test series should be arranged between England and Sweden in 1956 – three in Britain and three in Sweden.

He was quite impressed with Sweden and its riders and he wrote in his column:

The Swedish enthusiasm for the sport is terrific and it is easy to see why a claim might be made for a staging of a World Final over there. And what a country to travel around. Any touring side can include me – if they want me of course – because, rushed as we were, the whole trip was one of the most exciting experiences I've known.

A challenge match was scheduled to take place the next day in Oslo, Norway, between a Scandinavian team and a side comprising of the Australasians plus PC and Split Waterman. But changes were needed as Waterman was injured in the individual at Gothenburg, and Jack Young was also unavailable. Craven was made captain of the visitors, and it was a closely-fought contest which saw the visitors emerge as the winners with a 42-41 scoreline.

They left for Manchester the next morning, but were delayed at customs because of their bikes. This made for a mad dash in his Jowett Jupiter car from London to Manchester. It was a journey which didn't quite go according to plan, as Peter revealed in his column.

Although I stepped on it all the way, we were only at Newcastle-Under-Lyme at 6.30. Harold hopped out to phone Johnnie [Hoskins] *while I tried the rear lights which had been knocked about as we unloaded the machines. Still we pressed on and were about half a mile from the track when the petrol ran out!*

Suddenly a taxi came along, Harold pushed me into it, shouting that I was to send some petrol back with the taxi driver. This I did when I got to Belle Vue, but when the taxi driver got to the spot where Harold had been - he had gone! A Belle Vue supporter had stopped after seeing Harold sat in my car and had given him enough petrol to get into Belle Vue. I wonder just where that taxi man is right now with my petrol and a return fare?

Harold Jackson was one of the first men that Peter thanked over the public address system when he won the World Championship. It should be pointed out that Harold wasn't just Peter's mechanic, but also the pits mechanic for the Belle Vue team. These days, a top rider like Peter would have his own mechanic who would look after his bike and his alone. Quite often a modern rider never carries out his own mechanical maintenance; he leaves that to his personal mechanic. This was a luxury which was not available to Peter, and he was expected to look after his own bikes when he could.

Harold used to do all the bikes for the team, and he also prepared the bikes for Peter's World Finals as well, said Brenda. *Because he worked on the team's bikes, quite often Peter would find that he would have to go to Belle Vue — after he had driven all night following a meeting — to sort out his bike. So he had to do a lot of his own maintenance. It was quite expensive for rebuilds, even in those days, as there was no sponsorship like there is now. In fact Peter used earn around £20 to £25 a week during his time at Belle Vue which was a good wage as the footballers were earning about £12.50.*

To give the reader some idea of what a night would be like for a mechanic like Harold in the pits, Peter paid this tribute to him in his column. As the work began to mount up following their return from Sweden and Norway, Harold also had to make preparations for an historic trip, as Peter explained:

In the pits I changed into my leathers while Harold started to work on the machine I wrecked in Sweden. During the meeting more work began to pile up – Fred Rogers bent his bike frame, Arthur Wright 'blew' a motor, Peter Williams did likewise, so you will understand why Harold had to work solidly through Saturday night – after a rush back from Sweden – for everyone of those machines had to be loaded to leave Belle Vue for Poland at 10 o'clock on Sunday morning.

For this I give Harold my own Oscar for mechanics, because he did get those bikes finished and down to the airport in time.

Just minutes after stepping down from the famous Wembley tractor following his victory lap, he was approached by enterprising European promoters who were eager to book him for an appearance in their country. However, his Belle Vue boss, Johnnie Hoskins, and captain Ken Sharples – who was also the Speedway Riders' Association chairman – had already made arrangements for the Aces to travel behind what was then called 'The Iron Curtain' to race in Poland. Poland was part of the old Soviet Union, but the nation has always been one of the sport's major countries. But in 1955, such a tour was a groundbreaking undertaking as no British club had ever toured in an Eastern Bloc country since the war.

In Poland they call speedway racing *Zuzel,* which roughly translated means cinders. These days the nation is one of the sport's leading countries, and since the fall of the Soviet regime in 1989, speedway in

Poland has made great strides. However, in the Fifties it was a different story: there were political tensions between the West and the Soviet Empire which was ruled by Communist Russia. The Cold War was beginning to drop to its lowest temperature as the nuclear arms race began to gather pace, and the socialist countries became an unknown quantity as the Soviet Empire closed its borders. Therefore, a trip to Poland was indeed an adventure, as no one really knew what to expect as the country had not been free since they were invaded by Nazi Germany at the beginning of the Second World War.

We were very anxious about Peter and the Aces team going to Poland, because of the Iron Curtain – it was fear of the unknown really, said Brenda. *But Peter wasn't worried about it – nothing worried him – and I don't think the rest of the boys were worried about it either. But Ron Johnston was nearly arrested as soon as he stepped off the plane because he produced a camera. I think they were fearful of Westerners because of the Cold War.*

In his column Peter played down the incident as he seemed to realise there was more at stake here than just a visit from a British speedway team. Since the closing of the borders, there was very little information coming out of Eastern Europe and what did emerge was monitored by the governments.

From Brussels we got to Prague and our first glimpse under the edge of this Iron Curtain. And what did we see? Cheerful people collecting baggage, taking us through customs and hoping that we would enjoy our short stay in their city. Nobody stopped us wandering about, and the only time any interest was taken in our movements came when Ron Johnston decided to try out his cine camera on the airplanes around the landing strip. Then an airport policeman waved his hand to disapprove, but that could happen on any airport anywhere in the world.

As well as Peter and Johnston, the rest of the party were Ken Sharples, Dick Fisher, Bob Duckworth, Peter Williams, Fred Rogers and Arthur Wright from Bradford. Johnnie Hoskins was joined on the managerial team by Jack Fearnley – who was the manager of the entertainments side at Belle Vue – and, of course, Harold Jackson. At Prague they met Austrian riders Fritz Dirtl and Jozef Kamper, who were involved in the meeting at Wroclaw, and also Bohdan Lubinski of the Polish Motor Federation was also on hand to meet them and fill them in on latest developments about the tour.

The unloading of the bikes allowed the party to spend some time in the Czechoslovakian city, and they decided to take in a film show. The main feature was of some puppets with squeaky voices which amused Harold no end. So much so that he began to mimic them which didn't go down too well with the rest of the audience, and their visit 'ended sooner than we thought it should'.

They took the train to Wroclaw in Poland and they arrived in the early hours of the morning. The team were greeted with a lot of enthusiasm by the locals and when Peter emerged from his hotel room, a fruit seller was so pleased to see him that she gave him most of her fruit.

They were made very welcome and they raced in front of massive crowds, Brenda said. *When they went out they were followed everywhere by a secret policeman, but what they did was split up and go off in different directions so he couldn't follow them! None of the riders were paid – only in kind. By that I mean that they were given a beautifully cut glass vase which was the equivalent of what their pay would have been for a match at Belle Vue. All the equipment was owned by the state, so when Peter wanted to swap race-jackets with one of the riders he wasn't allowed to. This didn't bother Peter; he gave him the Aces' race-jacket anyway.*

The Aces' management had wondered what had happened to their famous Ace of Clubs race-jackets, but when inquiries were made, the incident was shrouded in a mystery of Cold War thriller proportions.

The meeting was a sell-out, with 60,000 people packed into the arena, and an estimated figure of a further 20,000 locked outside hoping that a seat would become available. It was reported that such was the attraction of the British team, that the stadium was half full by

3.00 p.m. that afternoon, even though the meeting was not due to get under way until 7.30 p.m. The results were broadcast to the throng of people outside the stadium. Belle Vue took part in a triangular tournament at Wroclaw, against teams from Poland and Austria. The Aces won the match with 38 points, Poland was second with 21 and the Austrian team, Motor Rennklub, was a distant third with just 12. Bradford guest Arthur Wright top-scored for the Manchester club with 12 while Peter secured 11 points.

The second match took place in the capital, Warsaw. This city had suffered heavy bombardment during the Second World War, and it was where the infamous Jewish ghetto was established. Significantly, the city had been in the news earlier that year as, on 14 May 1955, the so-called 'Warsaw Pact' was signed there. This was a defence alliance which was established by Albania, Bulgaria, Czechoslovakia, East Germany, Hungary, Poland, Romania and the Soviet Union, as a response to West Germany joining NATO. It was another indication that tensions between the East and West were gathering pace.

Belle Vue won the second match at Warsaw 66–42, and Peter led the scores for the Aces with 16 points, and he received good support from Johnston with 14 points, Sharples 11 and Peter Williams scored 9 points. Sharples and Johnston stood down from their final rides to allow Fisher and Brand the opportunity to have their first and only rides on the tour. For the Poles, Wlodz Szwedrowski impressed with a 16-point total.

Szwedrowski was the top Polish rider and as he revealed in his autobiography, *Na Ostrym Wirazu,* (which roughly translated means 'A Sharp Reaction/Reply') he was determined to beat one of the English riders – in particular Peter Craven. He was soundly beaten by the Aces' number one in the first race when he passed the Pole 'as though I was a novice'. He admitted that he was annoyed because he felt that Craven wasn't going very fast when he passed him. They were due to meet again later in the match, so Szwedrowski was keen to get his revenge.

I studied Craven carefully and decided that his abilities had been somewhat exaggerated, he observed. *But whether they were exaggerated or not, he was* the World Champion – not me. As far as entering the straights was concerned I felt that I could do better than Craven. His precision often failed him and every fraction of a second counted – Craven lost too much time. I began to realise that if all went well I could match Craven. I was determined to win!

After the interval I could sense the crowd anxiously waiting for my duel with Craven. I gated remarkably well, but Craven was right behind. I felt nervous because I was not sure where the attack was to come. Craven was level with my back wheel lurking like a tiger. After the first lap I saw the crowd again. They were roaring with frenzy. My nerves were strung like steel wires. If only I could hold out and have full control over my machine so as not to lose a tenth of a second.

Taking no notice of being sprayed with cinders, he ripped off his goggles to improve his vision. I sensed that Craven was getting furious. Yes furious! But he managed to control himself. When we crossed the line Craven was some fifteen yards behind me, he was very calm and composed. There was such a roar from the crowd when I got off my machine that I could not hear what was being said to me. The first to congratulate me for winning the race was Craven. It was very noble of him and I am sure the crowd appreciated his sporting gesture.

Poland had not seen the last of England's top rider, as he would return again and enhance his reputation further. And it appeared that he had enjoyed his first trip behind the Iron Curtain.

Warsaw is impressive, wrote Peter in Speedway News. That is the word for it. The population is about a million people – all housed – and yet 80 per cent of the city was destroyed by bombing during the war. We saw the huge stadium built by the Poles in just 10 months where 80,000 people will be seated when they watch football, athletics and other sports. The Poles – rightly, I thought – pointed with pride to their new 'Palace of Science,' a skyscraper of a building nearly 900-feet high, and to the Warsaw Zoo which lost all its animals during the early days of the war, but has since been replenished after a lot of hard work.

During the return journey the team were delayed at Prague because of their machines, and when they arrived at Brussels they found that they had missed their flight. After an overnight stay they boarded a flight to

Amsterdam, where among the passengers were some pheasants that were bound for a zoo in Britain. Peter was keen that a return tour for the Polish riders should be arranged so they could experience at first hand what British speedway was like. He had enjoyed the experience, and also the role he played in pioneering new speedway boundaries.

In the *Speedway Gazette*, Johnnie Hoskins also gave his account of the Aces' trip and wrote:

Our riders were made so welcome it was embarrassing in the extreme. We had the best rooms in the best hotels. The food was strange to us, but it was tasty and plentiful. We were toasted, feted and our every request was granted if humanly possible. 'Our English friends are happy. Yes?' was the frequent inquiry. Our lads were a credit to Britain. Well dressed, well behaved, courteous and modest.

One of our biggest laughs was at the Sports Platz, a magnificent concert hall in Wroclaw. A char woman had just finished polishing the stage when Ken Sharples grabbed my hat, rushed up and gave us a crazy dance. The woman went after him with her mop, and we didn't need an interpreter to understand what she was saying!

I'm proud of the fact that I took the Aces to Poland, said Jack Fearnley of that historic tour. *It was the very first visit of a British club side which led to the great relationship between the PZM [Polish Speedway's governing body] and the BSPA that exists today. Peter was in the team and he was marvelled at by our Polish friends, as was all of our team of that day. Peter's World Championship triumph was fully merited and he was idolised by the Belle Vue supporters.*

The role of a World Champion can be a varied and interesting one – especially off the track as Peter soon discovered. His new status brought an opportunity to be on a panel of judges at a beauty contest. He attended the annual ball held by the Leeds Speedway Social Club, and joining him on the judges table was Mrs Eddie Rigg, Keith Milner and another Peter Craven. This other 'Peter Craven' was a local journalist who covered motor sport. However, champion Peter presented the first prize to Miss Shirley Smart.

Peter also presented the prizes at the Wilmslow Cycle Speedway club for their 'Skid-Kid' team. When he handed out the awards, he was persuaded to give them a demonstration of the skills he displayed with the Prestbury Chads. However he crashed and sustained a minor injury to his back, but it didn't prevent him from getting back on and having another go. Earlier in the day, the Longsight and District Supporters' Club presented Peter with a beautifully engraved canteen of cutlery in appreciation of his efforts in bringing the World title to Manchester.

Through all the praise, the plaudits and the attention that came with being World Champion, Peter never forgot his good manners or his roots. Oates recalled another incident which illustrated that being a World Champion Speedway rider did not change him.

He had a Jowett Jupiter sports car which he bought from me, and my wife was wearing a full plaster cast because she had injured her back, he said. *We were living over the shop, and she was trying to clean the front step – because we are very proud of our clean front steps up here in the north – when Peter came by. He saw what she was trying to do and stopped her and cleaned the step for her. So here was a World Champion, on his hands and knees, cleaning the front step!*

In spite of being World Champion, Peter had no plans to race during the winter. Instead, along with his brother Brian, he planned a fitness programme that he described as 'kill or cure for the Craven brothers'. However, he did put in some laps around Ainsdale, where the other riders were keen to learn from the World Champion.

'That feels more like fame to me than winning the World Championship,' said Peter of his colleagues seeking some advice from him, 'because it only seems a couple of years ago that I was falling all over those Sands myself!'

It had been a year to remember for Peter Craven, and also a better season for the Aces, who finished in the runners-up spot behind Wimbledon in the National League Championship. As a new season dawned, Peter faced another new challenge as reigning World Champion, while Belle Vue sensed that the glory days could be back.

Four

THE ACE OF ACES

Making a successful defence of the World Individual Speedway Championship is not an easy task. In the sport's seventy-five-year history, only eight riders have managed to retain the title. But Peter would not have to suffer the embarrassment of not qualifying for the World Final like Freddie Williams did in 1954, as he was seeded directly through to the big night at Wembley. When he was asked about his thoughts on being seeded direct to the Final during a pre-season practice session at Hyde Road, he replied: 'I shall probably lose £100 in prize money, but it is worth double that to be free of the worry of fighting for the honour of being at Wembley.'

This left Peter free to concentrate on his racing with Belle Vue. It should be pointed out that at this stage he had still only completed two full seasons as a professional speedway rider, and only four years had passed since he made his tentative debut for Liverpool.

During the winter many debates and discussions took place about the future of the sport in Britain. Many theories and ideas were put forward such as handicapping the top riders, promotion and relegation between the First and Second Divisions, an amalgamation of the two divisions, a ban on foreign riders, and even a league that would feature top clubs from Sweden. In the end only promotion and relegation was put into operation – much to the disappointment of many who favoured an amalgamation of the two divisions.

There were very real indications that all was not well in the top division when West Ham closed. Poole was persuaded to step up from the lower league, but this was a quick fix for a problem that was growing as each month passed by.

All this made little difference to Peter Craven whose job at Belle Vue was the same: score as many points as possible. Only this year he would feel the extra responsibility of being the World's number one rider which meant that he was expected to win more races, and other riders would be trying that much harder to lower his colours because of his status. This was a situation that PC was only too aware of as he revealed in his column in *Speedway News*:

Winning the World Trophy is going to mean plenty of hard work besides the cheers and the champagne. Before that final night Peter Craven was just another member of the Belle Vue team – with a reasonable chance of collecting average points – and if he didn't, the fans and the critics didn't notice very much.

Now it seems I've got to be good all the time – there is the worry. Home riders think it is just dandy to beat the champion, but the fans think a champion should win every race and if he doesn't they wonder how the heck he became champion! That's why winning the trophy means hard work.

The Aces team was almost unchanged from the one that graced the British tracks in 1955, except that New Zealander Ron Johnston had decided not to return and was a non-starter. Not that this seemed to worry boss Hoskins as he believed that with Dick Fisher, Peter Williams and Maurice 'Slant' Payling in the side, their youthful exuberance would see them through. But in the final analysis the Aces missed the points scored by the Kiwi and they were not the force that they had been during the previous season. Therefore, Johnston made a return to the Vue in July and celebrated with a maximum as the Aces defeated Birmingham 45-39.

It has been suggested that Johnston would regularly threaten to remain in New Zealand and not to return to the British League. This diversion was one that the Kiwi believed would put him in a stronger financial position. While this was not made public knowledge, it was widely believed that Peter never received his true financial worth from Belle Vue because of his team-mate's annual shenanigans.

One of Peter's early season engagements was a Golden Helmet match race encounter against Wimbledon's former World Champion, Ronnie Moore. To give it its official title, the British Match Race Championship was left vacant at the end of the 1955 season as its holder, Jack Young, was injured. Therefore, the Speedway Control Board was required to nominate two competitors for the competition's first staging of the year. Who better than the reigning World Champion Craven, and the previous year's number one, Moore? In fact Moore had been heavily involved in the match race title during 1955, and he was due to face Young when the Aussie had to withdraw. Technically speaking Moore was the holder by default – which the SCB were eventually forced to acknowledge.

The Match Race Championship was a major event in the British calendar. It was always contested by two riders – the holder and the challenger – and usually staged on a monthly basis. The challenger would be nominated by the SCB. The winner of each leg would be decided by the best of three races, and it was held over two legs. Each rider would be given the opportunity to ride in the competition on his home track, but if the contest was all square after two legs, then a third would be staged at a neutral track.

The first leg of the Craven-Moore encounter was staged at Wimbledon's Plough Lane track, and this was a circuit that was not among Craven's favourites. Predictably he lost 2-0, but he put the less than fit Kiwi – who was riding with a wrist injury – under a lot of pressure. There was no stopping The Mighty Atom at Belle Vue as he reversed the tables and won 2-0, forcing a decider at Ipswich which he lost 2-1. It was Peter's first taste of this prestigious competition, and while he was a loser on this occasion, as his career progressed he would be no stranger to the tournament.

Johnnie Hoskins was successful in negotiating a deal that brought a Polish team over to Britain for a tour. They arrived at Belle Vue and surprisingly ran the Aces very close, losing 49-47. Poland's Wlodz Szwendrowski defeated Peter – his only defeat of the night. Poland made a favourable impression despite losing at both Wimbledon and

1 *Right:* Peter Craven aged thirteen.

2 *Below:* The Prestbury Chads Cycle Speedway Team. Brian Craven is sat on the bike, with Peter to his immediate left.

3 *Above:* From left to right, Peter, Brian and their father Ben pose with the JAP machine that they began using at the Ainsdale Sands training track.

4 *Left:* Peter leads the way on the Ainsdale Sands.

5 *Left below:* More action from Ainsdale as Peter leads another trainee, believed to be Tommy Murphy. Notice the cars parked by the track in the background.

6 The Liverpool Chads, 1951. From left to right: Team mechanic, Pete Robinson, Alf Webster, Buck Whitby, Harry Welch (on machine, captain), Len Read, Reg Duval, Peter Craven, Bill Griffiths, George Newton and Phil hughes (team manager).

7 *Left:* Peter powers along the straight at Liverpool's Stanley stadium.

8 *Below:* An early shot of Peter on the edge of his balance while riding for the Liverpool Chads.

9 *Left:* This is believed to be one of the first photographs taken of Peter in a Belle Vue race-jacket.

10 *Below left:* Peter in his army uniform with a film actress. Every effort was made to identify the lady, but attempts were unsuccessful. It would seem that she was one of the budding actresses from Pinewood Studios' 'Rank Charm School'.

11 *Below right:* Peter is presented with a trophy on the occasion of scoring his first maximum from Frank Maclean. It was said that Maclean was embarrassed to present him with such a small cup for his first full maximum.

12 Peter leads West Ham's Jack Young and Willie Nelson on his way to establishing a new track record on 8 May 1954.

13 Peter and Dick Fisher greet some of the fans after the match. Peter is seen talking here after spotting some of his former army colleagues.

14 The 1955 World Championship qualifying round at Belle Vue. From right to left: Peter Craven, Ron Johnston, Fred Rogers, Trevor Redmond.

15 Peter leads for the Aces.

16 *Right:* Up and away – Peter leaves the starting gate at Belle Vue.

17 *Right below:* The proud Craven family assemble to celebrate Peter's 1955 World Championship victory. From left to right: Brian, Brenda, Joan, Peter, George Woodall (married to Pat), Pat, and Peter's parents, Edna and Ben.

18 *Below left:* The Belle Vue Aces team return from Poland after their successful trip in 1955. From the front: Ken Sharples, Arthur Wright, Peter, Fred Rogers, Peter Williams, Dick Fisher, Ron Johnston, Jack Fearnley, Bob Duckworth and Johnnie Hoskins.

19 *Below right:* Peter with his mother, Edna, and the World Championship trophy he won in 1955. This photo was the first meeting at Belle Vue after Peter was crowned Champion of the World.

20 Peter shakes hands with Sweden's Ove Fundin before another classic match race.

21 Belle Vue Aces, the 1958 Britannia Shield Champions. From left to right, back row: Bob Duckworth, Peter Williams, Derek Maynard, Dick Fisher, Maurice 'Slant' Payling and Johnnie Hoskins. Front row: Ron Johnston and Peter Craven.

22 Ron Johnston (left) and Peter return with the trophy of Johnnie Hoskins' burnt hat on the end of the flag pole carried by Peter. This was a regular piece of entertainment that always took place when Hoskins was in charge at Hyde Road.

23 The England team, 1958. From left to right, back row: Ron How, Jimmy Squibb, Dick Bradley, Arthur Forrest, Brian Crutcher. Front row: Mike Broadbanks, Peter Craven, Ken McKinlay.

24 Peter at his spectacular and brilliant balancing best as he bursts between the Oxford duo of Gordon McGregor and Roy Bowers (on the outside) in 1960. This photo was taken by Peter Morrish, who is now the Conference League co-ordinator, and the photo won an award in 1960.

25 Skipper Peter Craven leads the England team out for the very first staging of the World Team Cup Final in the Ullevi Stadium, Gothenburg, Sweden in 1960. He is accompanied by the team manager, Ronnie Greene, and his other team-mates in view are Ken McKinlay, Nigel Boocock and George White.

26 Peter leads Ove Fundin in Austria, but note that Fundin is on the grass following some pretty determined riding from the Englishman.

27 Peter Craven, Leon Leat and Arne Pander pictured in Austria for the International Pairs Championship in 1960.

28 Soren Sjosten and Peter Craven. Sjosten was considered to be another Craven because of his similar style of riding.

29 Peter and Dick Fisher discuss tactics before another match for Belle Vue.

30 Peter Craven, with his face mask pulled down, looks for the opposition while he is in perfect control.

31 Peter leads Ove Fundin during one of their many memorable clashes.

Left: 32 Peter took over as the captain of Belle Vue in 1962.

Right: 33 Peter poses with the spoils of a champion, including the 'Winged Wheel' World Championship trophy and the Golden Helmet.

34 Peter Craven and Ronnie Moore, flanked by Oxford promoter Dickie Worth (left) and the sportswriter Don Clarke, walk to the starting gate at Oxford before the start of another Golden Helmet Match Race. (Photo courtesy of the *Fleet News Agency*)

35 Peter is congratulated by the film star Norman Wisdom following his victory in the 1962 World Individual Speedway Championship.

36 Sweden's Ove Fundin (left) and Peter Craven shake hands before the start of another match race duel.

37 Poignantly, as the reigning World Champion, Peter leads out the field for the introductions during his last World Final appearance at Wembley in 1963. (Photo courtesy of Nick Barber)

Left: 38 George Hunter (left) is pictured here with Peter in one of the last photographs taken of Peter before his fatal crash at Edinburgh, on 20 September 1963. (Photo courtesy of Speed-A-Way Promotions)

Right: 39 The rostrum for the 1988 Peter Craven Memorial Trophy. American Kelly Moran –also called 'The Wizard of Balance'- receives the trophy from promoter Peter Collins. In the foreground, from left to right are Kelvin Tatum (second), Brenda (Peter's wife) and Sam Ermolenko (third).

Birmingham before they returned to Hyde Road for an individual meeting. Craven was in blistering form as he swept aside the opposition to win the International Championship Cup with a 15-point maximum. But when he received the trophy from Manchester's Mayoress, Miss Regan, he handed the cup over to the Polish star, Szwendrowski, as a lasting gesture of friendship – not only between the two riders, but also Belle Vue Speedway and the Polish speedway nation.

Sponsorship in motor sport is very important – much more so now than it was in the 1950s. These days we are used to seeing footballer David Beckham endorsing a product, and the late double 500cc Grand Prix World Champion, Barry Sheene, was well known for his television adverts for the aftershave Brut – along with boxer Henry Cooper.

The American cigarette manufacturer Astorias was one of the few sponsors in speedway during this period. They put their name to an annual that was published about the sport, and also to a number of individual meetings in Britain. However, one of the requirements of the agreement was that the World Speedway Champion – and former champions too – would endorse their product in advertisements in the press. Therefore, Peter was seen in the pages of *Speedway Star & News* as saying: 'Astorias are so different – so satisfying.' Of course all this was before the real risks of smoking had come to the fore. It was especially surprising to see Peter involved in this as those who were close to him knew that he didn't smoke.

In those days there was no sponsorship at all for the riders and very little publicity, recalled Brenda. *Astorias cigarettes being the rare exception, and they sponsored a meeting at Belle Vue each year. It was accepted practice at that time that each year the World Champion advertised Astorias, thus promoting some publicity for speedway. Peter (and the rest of the champions) did receive a small fee for appearing in the advertisement. Peter never smoked – he was more than happy with a cup of tea.*

They're all sponsored now, and the riders were never sponsored in those days, Leon Leat recalled. *Those black leathers that Peter used to wear used to have extra padding on the shoulders, elbows, knees and so on, and they were really difficult to clean after a night's racing. It was suggested that he should approach the people who made the leathers to supply some cleaning equipment as a sponsorship arrangement. But we never heard anything. Now the riders have lots of sponsors.*

Peter maintained his form from the previous season instead of making great strides. His early season form was disappointing, and this was possibly due to the new tyre that was brought in – the tempestuous Johnston refused to use it during a visit to Wimbledon. However, PC got to grips with it and returned to the kind of form that accelerated his rise up the score charts. He was easily the Aces' top scorer and he also featured in England's 57–51 victory over Australasia in the Third Test at Poole.

In a memorable meeting in which he scored 15 points, it was his partnership with Ken McKinlay that proved to be very effective as they scored 27 points out of a possible 30 for almost an invincible performance. Peter was awe-inspiring as he weaved his way through the traffic in heat 4 to join McKinlay at the front. Fittingly it was Craven and McKinlay who clinched victory for the home nation with a 5–1 in the last race. It was an all-round team performance which saw the Belle Vue favourite generously loan his machine to England skipper Brian Crutcher in heat 10. England completed a 3–0 whitewash over their antipodean rivals.

When it came to the World Final at Wembley on 22 September, it was Sweden's Ove Fundin who the sport's experts were tipping as a probable winner. Once again there were some who were writing off the defending champion's chances.

Following the conclusion of the first race, it looked as though Craven would once again prove all the critics wrong as he stormed to victory over Ronnie Moore and the much-fancied Fundin. And as Eric Linden observed in his report in *Speedway Star*, there was no way that he was going to give up the title without a fight: 'Craven is riding with all the thrills his style brings. He looks to be down at every bend – it is obvious that champion Craven isn't going to lose this title of his easily.'

In his second race he dived inside Brian Crutcher and hit the front. Despite his best efforts, Crutcher could not make any impression on the Aces rider, but then disaster struck. On the final bend, the champion's engine blew and its groan of agony reverberated around the Empire Stadium. Crutcher cruised through for a win followed by Barry Briggs. But a ray of hope appeared when Alan Hunt retired from the race with mechanical difficulties of his own, so Peter was gifted a consolation point for third place.

A poor gate in his third race left him having to battle past Olle Andersson and Peter Moore, but he was unable to find the necessary speed to power past his fellow countryman, Arthur Forrest, which meant he had scored 6 points from three starts. A successful defence of his title seemed unlikely at this stage, as he trailed Fundin, Forrest, Ken McKinlay and Crutcher who all had 7 points each. Another defeat at the hands of McKinlay meant that a rostrum place also seemed unlikely. However, he won his last race over his Aces' team-mate, Dick Fisher, and found himself facing Arthur Forrest in a run-off to determine third place. Craven briefly got his nose in front of the Bradford rider but, just as before during their earlier encounter, he didn't have the speed to make the pass stick.

Peter Craven finished in fourth place on a night when Fundin won his first World Championship – the Super Swede never dropped another point after his opening heat defeat at the hands of the little Englishman. Ronnie Moore was second again. The title had slipped away from Peter's grasp, but he put in a sterling defence which was especially admirable when he had to swap to his second machine which was visibly slower than his preferred first choice – he set the fastest time of the night with his opening race win. Although disappointed, ever the sportsman in defeat, he said: 'There's always another year.'

However, there was already some controversy brewing before the dust had settled on the Wembley final, when it was discovered that neither Craven nor his in-form club-mate Fisher, were to be included in the England team that was due to race in Sweden in an international Test series. It transpired that Johnnie Hoskins had refused to release the Aces duo because he wanted them to be available for the remaining league matches.

But Craven patriotically said: 'It isn't finished yet. I don't forget the fact that I owe what I am to Belle Vue, but there is a question of England's prestige at stake.'

Eventually, Craven joined a makeshift England team in the 'land of the lakes,' who were still missing Crutcher, Forrest and Fisher. The Swedes viewed the tourists – Craven apart – as a reserve team and thumped them accordingly, 3-0. Peter top scored in the Third Test at Stockholm with 13 points, but England were still defeated heavily 69-39. In fact, it seemed that only Craven and Ken McKinlay offered any real resistance to a rampant Swedish team whose best performance was a whopping 71-37 hammering over the English in theSecond Test at Ostermalm – where Craven and McKinlay scored 8 points each.

At the end of the season Peter had another opportunity to win the British Match Race Championship, when he was nominated as the challenger for his British rival, Brian Crutcher. Despite using his home track knowledge to the full in the first leg, Crutcher lost the championship to PC when it went to a decider at Norwich and he lost the encounter 2-0. Said Crutcher of their battle to be the top Brit:

He was a tremendous competitor, but the rivalry between us was just because we both wanted to be the top scorer. I don't want to single out riders, but there were some riders around in the Fifties who were hard riders and they wouldn't give you any room. They had a ruthless streak – a win at all costs way of riding. But Peter wasn't like that, he was a very fair rider and he was safe. He had so much ability that he didn't need to be a hard rider. The promoters I raced for were great showmen, and of course, Belle Vue had Johnnie Hoskins who used to burn his hat and so on. So there was this rivalry that was built up in the press a bit between Peter and me, but it was no more than friendly rivalry.

By the end of the season Belle Vue had finished fifth out of seven teams during a difficult campaign. Brian Craven had also made some promising appearances for the Aces during the season, as they fought to find a winning combination. Peter actually ended the season with a slight increase in his league average, and despite the World Championship disappointment, he had won both the Champagne Derby and The Supporters' Club individual meetings.

Nonetheless, the most important date in his diary for 1956 was 17 October at St Lawrence's Church, Everton, where he married Brenda Williams – his long-time sweetheart. His brother, Brian, was his best man, and there was little doubt that this occasion was the highlight of his year.

Peter and Brenda were a lovely couple, recalled Joan, *they were a good match – soul mates. Everyone who met them liked them because they were so genuine; it was such a great shame that they had such a short time together.*

Barry and June Briggs were married on the same the day, and both couples enjoyed a honeymoon cruise to South Africa. Peter and Brenda both liked South Africa and enjoyed their stay in this colourful country. But apartheid was in operation at this time, and the country could be troublesome due to this much-hated form of discriminative legislation. As a result it wasn't wise to go out alone at night.

Nonetheless, the speedway riders gamely got on with entertaining the crowds, and Peter was also joined in Africa by not only Briggs, but also the charismatic Swede Olle Nygren. However, Peter was in devastating form in South Africa and left his opponents chasing his rapidly disappearing back wheel. At one point he had fifty-one consecutive victories to his name – one magazine said that he completed seventy-two races before he tasted defeat – and he established a new track record and one lap record at Pretoria. Furthermore, while racing for the West Rand Rockets, he astonished the crowd with a stunning victory over Briggs. The Kiwi made the gate and drove into the first bend at a terrific pace, but PC rode flat out around the outside and swept into the lead. Briggs put the pressure on him, but every challenge was resisted with relative ease.

Nygren, though, was baffled by the way that Peter was so fast and dominated his races. Therefore, as he thought that he must have been using something special, he decided to take matters into his own hands in a bid to discover the secret that was making him seemingly unbeatable. He said:

He won everything and the rest of us got a bit fed-up. Barry Briggs and I thought that he must have been cheating so we nicked his bike one night, as we were determined to find out what was inside. We stripped it down, we looked and we checked it and found nothing – everything was standard. We thought that he had a high compression or special cams. We ran 13 or 14 high compression, but when we took Peter's bike down we couldn't believe it because he was running just 11! So we thought and knew that it wasn't the bike – so it had to be him. He was absolutely unbelievable. We couldn't touch him – it was just him and he rode so well. I shall never forget that.

While Peter was establishing himself as the Ace in Africa, in Britain the British League seemed to be in serious difficulties. A host of clubs closed through one reason or another, these included Wembley, Poole and Birmingham. Therefore, the decision was finally taken to amalgamate the remaining clubs into one league – tough times were ahead. Speedway in Britain faced even more problems when the league programme was delayed because of a fuel crisis following the Suez Canal Crisis. At this point the future for speedway racing was looking decidedly bleak.

However, there was some excitement when it was announced that Liverpool intended to re-open for business. Ex-Chads' favourite Reg Duval was behind the new initiative to resurrect the Liverpool Chads Speedway team, and along with his wife they put their life savings into resurrecting the stadium as a speedway venue. Duval decided to ditch the nickname 'Chads' and replace it with the 'Eagles'. Craven and the legendary leg trailer Oliver Hart were on hand to advise the enthusiastic Duval on the new track, and Harry Welch was installed as their team manager.

Instead of embracing a new track, the Promoters Association of that time did not appear to help Duval in his venture. He was frustrated in his search for riders, and as the Association collected a booking fee for every league rider that was used for a non-league track, Duval quickly found that there was very little financial benefit – especially when he paid out the dreaded Entertainments Tax.

Liverpool were to operate on an open licence, and Belle Vue saw the benefit that the venue could be for their young riders like Derek 'Tink' Maynard, Peter Williams, Brian Craven – he retired mid-way through the season due to a leg injury – and Slant Payling. It would give them the opportunity to get more competitive racing away from the hustle and bustle of National League competition. However, a lack of riders eventually forced Duval to close the circuit after the Eagles had raced successfully in a series of challenge matches. One of these saw Ivan Mauger ride for Oxford when he was loaned by Wimbledon for the fixture.

Nonetheless, the first meeting to be staged under the new promotion was the Liverpool Easter Trophy individual event. Graciously, Ipswich promoter Arthur Franklyn released Peter from his booking at a prestigious meeting at Foxhall Heath, so that he could ride in his home town. PC was in scintillating form despite carrying a knee injury he had sustained in South Africa, and he raced to an unbeaten 15-point maximum to win the meeting. A crowd reported to be in the region of 11,000 people saw their local star sweep all before him, and his spectacular charge around the outside of Peter Williams left the Stanley throng under no illusions of how special their little hero had become.

Johnnie Hoskins had largely kept faith with his team from the 1956 campaign, although Ken Sharples was replaced by Ron Johnston as skipper. Sharples had decided to retire after sustaining an injury during 1956. This meant that Johnston, who was set to move to Birmingham, was retained. Johnston and Craven were catching all the headlines for their powerful spearhead at Belle Vue.

But for Peter it was a season when he established himself as unquestionably Belle Vue's number one rider, and also his country's top rider too. He was in excellent form, and he was virtually unbeatable around

Hyde Road. He led the Aces to a much-improved year when they finished as runners-up to Swindon – who had also won the Second Division championship the previous year. But while the league title may have eluded the Aces by just 1 point, the team won their first major trophy since Johnnie Hoskins took over when they lifted the Britannia Cup.

The competition saw the clubs split into north and south sections, and run on a league basis. The Aces won their group, while the Fundin-led Norwich Stars won the Southern section. Therefore, the two clubs met in a two-legged final. With the 1955 and the 1956 World Champions in opposition, it was a match-up that was destined to catch the imagination. The East Anglian region had been privileged to see the rivalry that was developing between the spectacular Englishman and the calculated and ruthless Swede.

Peter had a thing about Ove Fundin, believed Tony Mann. *He had the beating of Briggs and Ronnie Moore, but for some reason he found it harder getting the better of Fundin. Of course he did beat him, but I think he was his biggest rival.*

Nearby Yarmouth had re-opened on an open licence too, and they staged the East of Anglia Individual meeting where Fundin and Craven went head-to-head in a run-off for the title after they had both finished on 14 points. It was Fundin who won, despite the close attentions of the British number one who lost out after an over slide while chasing the man they called 'The Fox'. They met again in an East Anglia *v.* The Rest challenge match at the popular seaside venue, with the Belle Vue man sweeping to an unbeaten 15 points with two emphatic victories over Fundin. Craven was riding for The Rest who lost 50-46 to the East Anglians.

The first leg of the Britannia Trophy was held at Belle Vue, but the added star attraction was the British Match Race Championship clash between Craven and Fundin. 'The Wizard of Balance' had already made one successful defence of his title against New Zealander Barry Briggs, but this meeting between the World Champions of the last two years was looked upon as a major encounter. Craven and Fundin had both been in excellent form, and with the World Championship qualifying rounds having already started, many people saw this as an indication of who could win the 1957 World Championship.

Craven made good use of his home advantage with a 2-0 success over the Swede in the first leg. Fundin's engine had failed in the first race, and Peter was handed a gift win. However, Ove was in the lead as the two riders hit the first bend during the second race, but PC swept around him to take the lead and secure overall victory. During the match, the Aces were held to a 48-48 draw despite sparkling performances from Craven (17) and Johnston (13). With the second leg set for Norwich, the Aces were hoping to at least take an advantage with them to The Firs track.

Once again, as a warm-up to the main event, the second leg of the Craven *v.* Fundin Match Race challenge took place before the second leg of the Britannia Trophy. Peter won the first race, but Fundin turned on the style and forced a decider by winning the second leg 2-1. In the second race it looked as though Craven's outside line would provide the necessary speed to sweep around his challenger but, in a style that came to characterise their clashes, Fundin hugged the inside and won the race.

In the Trophy match, an exciting clash took place that saw the Aces pull off a surprise 50-46 victory. In a match that produced some close and memorable racing, Johnston was in inspired form as he led his team with 15 points, and he received solid support from Peter who scored 13 and Bob Duckworth who finished with a match-winning 10 points. It was Belle Vue's first piece of silverware since they won the National Trophy in 1949.

While the destination of the Britannia Cup may have been decided, Craven and Fundin had to renew their battle to decide who would win the British Match Race Championship at Southampton. The popular Craven won both races to retain the title at Banister Court. The critics saw this as a significant triumph, and they began to tip the Ace as a possible World Champion for that year.

The World Championship qualifying rounds were modified slightly in 1957. A series of nine qualifying rounds were staged, and the top 32 scorers would then progress to semi-finals staged at Belle Vue and Birmingham. Each rider would have two qualifying rounds to compete in at different tracks. As each club staged a round, no doubt the thinking behind this formula was to give each of the eleven National League tracks the potential of a World title money spinner.

Peter began his World Championship campaign by competing in a qualifying round at Swindon. He finished runner-up to Ian Williams with 14 points – dropping his only point to the eventual winner. He booked his place in the semi-final with a victory in his second round at Wimbledon with an unbeaten score and established a new track record of 64 seconds in his second race. Peter's Aces team-mate, Ron Johnston, and Briggs were equal second with 13 points each.

With Peter's semi-final at Belle Vue, he was not only the favourite to qualify for his fourth World Final, but also to win the meeting. He duly obliged on both counts, although he had to defeat Johnston in a run-off to make sure of taking the £75 first prize after the Belle Vue team-mates had both tied on 13 points each. The meeting was marred by terrible weather conditions, and also saw the elimination of Brian Crutcher from the World Championship hunt.

Unlike the previous years, this time Craven was tipped by many to take the World title and become England's first double winner. John Hyam, writing in *Speedway Star & News* said of the little Liverpudlian's chances: 'Craven's performances this season has been nothing short of top class. On his day he can win any event on any track.' And fellow columnist Howard Jacobi agreed, and added that he was England's only genuine World Championship hope. The editor, Eric Linden, wrote that he was a 'certain winner'. Almost all the staff on *Speedway World* agreed that little Craven would win his second World title, with journalist Peter Arnold observing: 'He is not affected by the occasion and has first class equipment.' Meanwhile, Peter himself was quoted in the *World* as saying: 'It's so open this year; so for an outsider I pick Olle Nygren.'

The opening heat brought together Peter and Fundin. The Final couldn't have begun with a better opener. Joining them was Scotland's Ken McKinlay and Rune Sormander from Sweden. Craven made a poor start; he couldn't get on terms with Fundin and had dropped his first point of the night. He finished third behind Australia's Jack Geran and Briggs in his next race which all but ended his Championship hopes.

He won his third outing, but a surprise defeat at the hands of Peo Soderman meant that his best hope was a place on the podium. With the final round of races to come, it was Fundin and Briggs who led the scores with 11 points each, Aub Lawson was third with 9 and Peter shared fourth with Sormander on 8 points. Peter won his last race, while Fundin defeated Lawson to establish a brace of run-offs to determine the medals for that year.

Fundin faced Briggs in a run-off to decide the 1957 World Championship. The Kiwi had already defeated Fundin once that evening; but this time he won more easily as Fundin crashed out and his defence of the title ended in the debris of the Wembley safety fence. The Kiwi received a mixed reception – not that Briggs cared, he was the champion and that was all that mattered. Peter then faced Lawson in a run-off for third. In a race that was befitting of a rider who had been in outstanding form for his club and a pre-meeting favourite, he won with a tapes to flag demolition of the Australian Lawson.

Peter ended a very successful season by finishing the year as the holder of the British Match Race Championship. He made a successful defence against Swindon's World Finalist, Bob Roger, even though it went to a decider at Norwich. He also won the Pride of the Midlands Trophy at Leicester with another full house and, with a league average in excess of 11 points, there was no doubt that he was England's top rider. He finished as both the league and Aces' top scorer with 272 points, and scored 8 full and 3 paid maximums.

While he may have had to settle for third place in the World Final, his popularity among the public made him the peoples' number one. *Speedway Star* ran a poll to find the most popular visiting rider among supporters in the country, and Peter was voted the top visitor. Furthermore, over the course of the season, the magazine ran a ranking system that consisted of journalists and other experts, who would vote for who they considered to be best rider during a given period of time. At the end of the season, PC finished top with 20 votes ahead of Southampton's Crutcher, and over one hundred ahead of World Champion Briggs.

On 3 November 1957, the Cravens celebrated the birth of their first child, Robert. As far as Peter and Brenda were concerned, all the polls and the honours bestowed upon Peter as a speedway rider took a very distant second place behind the joy and celebration they shared following the birth of their son. Peter was now a proud father, which he believed was more important than the exhilaration he felt when he was sliding a 500cc speedway bike around the tracks in the country. But the new responsibility of fatherhood did not bring about any thoughts of retirement.

As the new season began there seemed to be very little let-up in his performances on the track. Indeed, his new-found status as a father saw him begin his sixth season as an Ace in better form than ever before. He was unbeaten in four matches – including full maximums at home and away during their clashes with Oxford – and then after two matches in which he scored 12 points, he then ended the Britannia Shield campaign by racing unbeaten in three successive matches. Peter Craven was riding better than ever. Peter Williams often found himself paired with the in-form Ace, and although Craven was accommodating to his partner, Williams observed that Craven's natural ability enabled him the kind of freedom in a race that most riders only dream about.

I remember being in the first race at BV and winning it in the fastest time of the night, Williams recollected. *When I got back to the pits, I said Peter had let me win it, but Ken Sharples, and Ron Johnston said, 'don't you believe it; he was doing his best to catch you.' I think during the last two years that I rode at Belle Vue, I rode with PC as his partner in the races. He would let me choose what gate position I wanted. He wasn't fazed by gate positions; as long as his partner was happy – he was. Again, when I finished riding, I realised that the second strings didn't want to ride with him. Riding as his partner meant that you were up against Craven, Ronnie Moore, Jack Young, Brian Crutcher, Tommy Price etc. With Peter always high scoring, it was hard work for his partners. We would be side-by-side during a race, but then he would be off and away and he would say afterwards: 'Sorry, I couldn't wait for you.' What I enjoyed most was chasing after him, and trying to out-think him and pass him. I also loved the dash to the first corner with all the legs and elbows that were sometimes needed in the first corner.*

Peter's first defence of his British Match Race Championship was against the new World Champion, Barry Briggs. It was traditional that the reigning World number one was chosen as the first challenger of the season – if he wasn't already the holder of course. Peter won both legs, and also set a new track record at Belle Vue in the second race with 69.8 seconds. Briggs was swept aside and he also marvelled at the sensational early season form of the former World Champion in his column in *Speedway Star & News:*

Isn't Peter Craven flying this term! Those match race clashes with the little Belle Vue racer left me gasping. Peter certainly set a cracking pace, as the fact that he broke the Wimbledon and Belle Vue track records in successive days proves. There is no doubt about it, when it comes to two-man racing Peter is one of the shrewdest tacticians in the game.

The Belle Vue Aces remained largely unchanged from the side that almost won the league championship in 1957. After the usual will he won't he, is he going to retire ruse from Johnston, the Kiwi eventually took his place in the Manchester team saying that he was only interested in racing for the Aces that year. Bob Duckworth made it a heat leader trio that was a match for any of the others in the country, and with Williams and Dick Fisher also included in the side, champagne celebrations were expected to return to the Aces pack.

The first competition was the defence of the Britannia Shield. And after the qualifying rounds had been completed, the Aces had won every match and finished at the top of their group. Wimbledon had also achieved a similar success in their group. Therefore the Final was between the glamour club of the North and the glamour club of the South.

The Wimbledon Dons included New Zealand's World Champions Barry Briggs and Ronnie Moore in their side. By the time the Britannia Shield Final was staged, it was the Dons who were ahead of the much-fancied Aces in the table. In spite of the absence of Williams through a shoulder injury, the Aces put in a determined performance that was akin to the displays of the early post-war teams. They lost the first leg at Plough Lane by just 2 points, and then sealed victory at Hyde Road with a 10-point triumph to successfully defend their title. The star of the show at Wimbledon was Eddie Rigg, whose 10 points did much to keep the Aces within striking distance of Wimbledon for the return at the Zoo.

The Aces also won the National Trophy for the first time since 1949, with a 136-103 victory over Norwich. It was a cup double for the Aces, but injuries during the mid-season ended their hopes of a league title and they finished in fifth place in a year when Wimbledon won the league championship thanks largely to the return of Ronnie Moore in June.

Among the Wimbledon team during 1958 was a fresh-faced young rider from New Zealand who would go on to become one of the sport's greatest riders – Ivan Mauger. It was his first season in Britain, and as he revealed in a correspondence with the author, he was eager to listen and learn from the top riders of the day.

I was first over as a seventeen-year-old in 1958 and I travelled around a lot with Barry Briggs and Ronnie Moore. Of course, they were good friends with Peter so although Peter would never have remembered me, and probably never talked to me, I was often in the dressing room with Ronnie, Barry, and Peter, and all the other great riders of that era. I used to stand around pur-

posely listening to what they talked about, and trying to learn their reasons for doing all sorts of things connected with racing, such as getting ready to race and bike maintenance. It was really just a million things that a young rider needs to know.

Following the amalgamation of the two divisions, this brought Midland rivals Leicester to Hyde Road, and consequently took the Aces to them. Leicester proved to be a popular venue for Aces' supporters and riders. The track at Blackbird Road was far enough away to warrant an outing, and yet it wasn't a venue that required too much time devoted to travelling. Furthermore, the circuit always produced some fine racing and it was a favourite with Craven and the other riders – and would remain so until its closure in 1984. David Blinston was another recipient of Peter's generosity during his trip to Leicester, and soon discovered that his ability for speed was not just confined to the race track.

I went to see the Aces at Leicester, and I was in the pub wondering what I was going to do with myself once the pub had closed, because my train back home didn't leave until 1.15 in the morning. Then someone suggested I ask Peter for a lift. So I did and, to my delight, he agreed. He was a very nice chap, but I had a little bit to drink you see, so I had to stop off on the way for a call of nature – and Peter went bananas! I guess he was eager to get back, as we were home within an hour and a half! I don't think you could do the journey in that time even now. That was some going.

Blinston also recalled another incident at Leicester that proved that wee Peter had not forgotten his working-class background.

I found out that when racing at Leicester, after the meeting, he would sit down to a meal provided by Leicester. But before he sat down to eat he used to sit and talk to a very young girl – about three or four – and talk to her for a few minutes. That was typical of Peter, who although perhaps he was a bit of a brash Scouser, he never forgot his working-class roots.

Peter lost the British Match Race Championship for the first time since 1956 when Ove Fundin defeated the Englishman. It went to a decider at Poole, but the Swede won 2-0. It was not surprising that it took the clever Fundin to end Peter's long reign as the Golden Helmet holder, as up until that point very few riders has been able to lower his colours. These were the two in-form riders.

Much has been written about the rivalry between them, but it must be pointed out that there was no animosity between these superstars of speedway. The Swedish World Champion's popularity outside of Norwich was not very good, and this was brought to the fore when he met Craven. Peter's popularity was never questioned: he was personable, spectacular and entertaining, but above all, he was English. Most people agree that Fundin was his biggest rival, and he was also the rider that offered him his toughest challenge. But there is also a consensus of opinion that says that he was intimidated by the Swede. I find this idea unlikely, but what is clear is that Fundin employed a different approach to his racing and his tactics on the track.

Peter Williams observed that Fundin's tactics would ruffle Craven's feathers in a way that no other rider could as these were questionable tactics that went against Craven's sense of fair play.

When Peter raced against Ove Fundin, he hated being at the start line with him, said Williams. *Peter would come to the tapes, wait and stand still. That's how we did it. But Fundin would not keep still; rolling backwards and forwards and really looking to make a flyer. I have known Peter come back to the BV pit gate complaining that Fundin wouldn't keep still. Years later we would find out that there were always riders who would creep on the start line to get an advantage. It goes without saying that Peter felt that everyone should play by the rules.*

Craven was an instinctive and natural racer, while in contrast his rival was more calculating and he was uncompromising on the track. Some would say he was ruthless; but it is a well-known fact that Fundin's purpose on the track was to win – and he would concentrate all his efforts to be first past the chequered flag. PC's approach was much more relaxed. He wanted to win as much as the next rider, but he enjoyed his racing.

We had a lot of tough races together, and, of course, we were two of a kind because we were both there to win speedway races, said Fundin. *He was such an outstanding rider – there was no question about that. He wanted to win and he was very determined. He was always nice and friendly, but I'm not too sure that I was all that nice and friendly. But being a foreigner and all that, it was a different situation. He was a very clean rider, which you could not always say about some of the other riders, but you could always trust Peter. He wasn't one of those riders who would try and fence you. You could always trust him.*

The match races we had together I remember very well, but I wouldn't say that he was my main rival because there was Barry Briggs and Ronnie Moore as well. When we had those handicap races, there would always be him and I standing at the back and fighting it out. And we would be fighting it out amongst ourselves because we forgot about the others. Perhaps that's not very nice, but that's the way it was.

For some reason their careers were linked. They both made their World Final debuts in 1954; it was Fundin's last heat win in 1955 that made sure that PC won the World title. It was Fundin who relieved the World crown from PC in 1956, and now he had ended his reign as British Match Race Champion. Needless to say, their tussles on the track were always memorable, and their contests almost guaranteed the promoters an increase in their attendance. They were vastly different when they raced, and it was these two different styles of racing that guaranteed that sparks would fly when they met.

Following a season of indecision and confusion in 1957, Test matches were restored to the British calendar for 1958. Peter Craven was made captain of his country as England faced Poland in a three-match series. He felt that it was an honour to be able to lead his country into action, but it was no more than his talents deserved.

Almost three years had passed since Belle Vue first travelled to Poland, and now they were sending over a national team to take part in a Test series against England. But alas, the Polish team were no match for England on their own turf and were soundly whitewashed 3-0, with England never scoring less than 77 points. *Speedway Star* described it as a 'humiliation', but Peter was happy to be captain of a successful England team. He scored an 18-point maximum in the Second Test at Ipswich, and scored 47 points from the three matches to finish as his country's top scorer.

In a busy international season for the England team, Craven shared the captaincy with his rival Brian Crutcher during this year. As well as the series against Poland, they faced Australasia and Sweden, and then travelled to Sweden and Poland for a series in those respective countries. It was during the three-match series against the Swedes in Britain that Swindon's George White recalled a memorable incident during the Second Test at Norwich that illustrated just how talented Craven was.

At Norwich, Peter asked me if he could borrow my bike because we were both small riders. I hadn't being doing terribly well, but Peter went out on it and won a race. And I thought, 'oh, it must be me'. But he was a good captain and a really nice man, and he would always help you. He would advise us on what gear to use and the right lines and things like that, but I never dared borrow his bike. He was the most spectacular rider I have ever seen, and it was fantastic to watch him race. There has never been anyone else like him – he had incredible balance

By September 1958, he held track records at Swindon, Norwich, Wimbledon, Leicester, Oxford and Belle Vue. He set the fastest time of the season at Poole, and it was while he was defeating Ron How in a Match Race eliminator at Oxford that Eric Linden marvelled at his speed.

He had already been impressed by the Belle Vue rider's pace on a narrower tyre to match the record set by Ken Middleditch in 1956, when in his next race he took speed to another level for the magazine editor when he set a record of 63.4 seconds.

So there I am thinking that young Craven has done pretty well on a 354-yard circuit which is not the easiest in the country to ride, when blow me down the boy steps up again for another crack. But he doesn't nibble any fifths of a second off – oh no. Craven goes completely haywire and chops off two whole seconds!

Peter qualified comfortably for the World Final at Wembley, and he was red-hot favourite to regain the World Championship. He faced the defending champion, Briggs, in the opening race and quickly discovered that the track was not in the sort of condition one would expect for a meeting of such importance.

Aub Lawson took the lead but was passed by Briggs and then Craven. But in his pursuit of the Kiwi, Craven found bumps and holes all around the track. For a rider like PC who raced on the edge of balance, combined with his small frame, this was not a comfortable experience. He easily won his second race, but then suffered a disastrous third outing that saw him struggling at the back as he raced into the first bend, and then he was virtually filled in at every turn. His title hopes had evaporated into the dense dust that greeted his Wembley turns. But he didn't give up. While Ronnie Moore and Olle Nygren scrapped over the lead in heat 15, Craven kept a watching brief. Nygren took Moore so wide for the lead that by the time they had both recovered, Peter was through and in front and raced to victory. With a rostrum placing still in his sights, he faced Fundin in heat 19.

In front of a reported crowd of 61,000, the Swede passed Peter down the back straight and he hugged the white line while Peter persisted with his pursuit around the boards. His persistence paid off as he regained the lead on the third lap. Fundin was flustered by this audacious move on a difficult surface, and he almost crashed as the Ace flashed by.

Briggs retained the title with a faultless 15-point maximum with Fundin assured of second place with 13. Peter found himself lining up against Aub Lawson and Ken McKinlay in a run-off to decide third place. Lawson and Craven had met before for this final rostrum position in 1957. But this time it was Lawson who took the bronze after the track condition pitched first of all McKinlay over his handlebars, and then Peter also hit the deck after hitting a bump.

It was disappointing for Peter to finish in fourth with 11 points, but the track conditions came in for criticism from the riders. Ove Fundin said: 'This circuit is definitely not up to World Championship standards. Those bumps don't bear thinking about.' Fellow country-man Olle Nygren was also unhappy, and one magazine described his views as 'unprintable'.

Craven then led an England touring side for a three-match Test series in Sweden and behind the Iron Curtain to face the Poles. They lost the series in Sweden 2-1, although skipper Craven was in fighting form throughout the three matches scoring double figures in each match. In Poland the visitors won all three Tests, and Peter once again wowed the Polish supporters with an impressive display that saw him score 17 in the First Test, a maximum of 18 points in the second match at Rybnik, and another 17 points in the final Test at Wroclaw.

The touring team were Ken McKinlay, Dick Bradley, Ron How, Mike Broadbanks, Billy Bales and George White. The team manager was Vic Gooden and their mechanic was Ted Brine. They produced a patriotic performance despite the absence of Crutcher, who turned down the tour – another indication that he was becoming disillu-sioned with the sport. George White performed with some distinc-tion on the tour that included 13 points in the Third Test against the Swedes, and twice he collected 14 points in the first two Tests against Poland. He had some vivid memories of the trip.

I remember on one occasion during a match in Poland, it had been a really wet, wretched day. The cinders were really deep, and Peter used to race by putting his foot down when he started the turn and then trail his left leg. Well, because the cinders were so deep, he was able to leg trail as soon as he started to turn and that was brilliant to watch. He had such wonderful balance.

He was a real captain too and helped whenever he could. In Wroclaw I dropped a valve, and Peter insisted that I used his bike for the rest of the match. I really appreciated that gesture. But it was so wet at Wroclaw that the wooden board fence that they put up in this stadium had buckled. Dick [Bradley] crashed in one race and injured his left leg. He also cut his mouth so badly that he had to have something like 18 stitches. The Polish doctors wanted to keep him in, but he pleaded with Peter and me not to leave him behind. There were big crowds there for the three Tests, and we had a lot of fun on the tour.

As it would seem with all the top riders, Peter never let the conditions bother him. Frank Maclean recalled in *Websters Speedway Mirror 1972* that only once at the notorious track at Exeter did Peter consider giving in to the elements after a couple of poor rides that included a fall. He had arrived at the County Ground dog-tired after travelling down from Norwich. But when he heard the cheers of the crowd he said: 'They have paid to see me, and they deserve better than I am giving them.' Maclean goes on to record that he went out and rode at his spectacular best, but he didn't go out on the centre green to acknowledge the crowd's applause. Instead, after his final race he was found fast asleep in the car.

Peter faced Brian Crutcher in the Match Race Championship, but the weather prevented the decider from taking place and the challenge was meant to be held over until the following year. But during the winter it was decided that Crutcher should begin the season as the holder after all. It had been another successful season that also saw him win the Pride of the East Trophy at Norwich and the International Pairs with Ken McKinlay at St Austell. But that second World Championship still eluded him – although *Speedway Star & News* found that the tiny Craven had finished the season as the top-ranked rider for the second successive year by their panel of experts.

Despite several offers he chose to spend the close of season at home. As well as looking after his family he also spent the winter training novices on the Ainsdale Sands. But as a former World Champion, England captain and Belle Vue's superstar, he was often in demand for personal appearances.

He was not one for forgetting his roots, and in particular his humble cycle speedway beginnings. He was the president of the Wilmslow Hammers Cycle Speedway team, but he also attempted to support other clubs in the area if he thought that his presence would be of some benefit to them. Peter Williams recalled an occasion when he was all set to step in as a reserve replacement for his famous team-mate as a guest at a cycle speedway club.

On one occasion Peter was asked to present a trophy at a cycle speedway match at Cheadle, which was not many miles away. Peter didn't think he could make it, so I went as his deputy. But Peter turned up just in time to be greeted by a very enthusiastic crowd of cycle speedway supporters. Things like that remain with people all their lives.

At no point did his achievements go to his head. Vic White, who is now the Secretary of the Veteran Speedway Riders' Association, was himself a former rider and speedway promoter. He recalled an incident following a meeting at Wimbledon.

Belle Vue were racing at Wimbledon one evening in the Fifties, and after the meeting we waited outside the pits to speak to Peter, White recollected. *Along came Peter and he stopped to talk to us. My son Keith was not very old and I said to him: 'Do you know who this is?' He said 'Yes, it is Peter Moore!' Peter was very amused by this, and we all enjoyed a good laugh about it.*

During 1958, Peter Craven joined the committee of the Speedway Riders' Association. Ken McKinlay was also on the committee along with Australian Aub Lawson who was the overseas riders' representative. Cyril Brine was the chairman while Phil Clarke was the vice chairman. The 1958 Annual General Meeting was remembered for a constitutional change that was suggested by Lawson. He recommended that the SRA AGM should be held at the beginning of the season and not at the end. All the members agreed, and their AGM was held over until the following year.

In January 1959, the Secretary-Treasurer, Sid Singleton, informed Brine that he intended to step down from his post for personal reasons. The committee drew up a list of suitable applicants, and in April the former *Speedway Gazette* editor Cyril J. Hart accepted the post. Ronnie Moore took over from Lawson as the overseas representative. Cyril Hart, who now runs the *Fleet News Agency*, wrote a series of recollections for this book, and he recalled an Association meeting of particular interest to Hollywood fans.

As its secretary I always endeavoured to arrange meetings, not only when they were really necessary but at venues which required the least amount of additional travelling…not the easiest of tasks when riders were with clubs which were scattered all over the country.

On one urgent occasion Belle Vue were at Wimbledon on a Monday in a league match, in a cup tie at New Cross on the Wednesday, and Craven was booked for an individual meeting at Wembley on Thursday and would be in London for the week. That meant I would be likely to get the Dons big two, Ronnie Moore and Barry Briggs, their team-mate Chairman Cyril Brine, Danny Dunton, and a couple of others, and BV's Peter Craven together on the Tuesday evening. No problem with travelling, though our usual venue wasn't available, but Cyril's wife, Betty, kindly offered us to use the spacious lounge in their Borehamwood home.

The meeting went on a bit, we got through several packets of fags, and 'Salty' Brine eventually mentioned to Betty that a spot of supper wouldn't go amiss. Betty said that she was quite willing to provide some sandwiches and liquid refreshment, but as there were eight or nine of us and the meeting had been sprung on her she was unprepared. 'Why not take the boys over to the Grosvenor Restaurant by the film studios,' she said.

We were all chatting away, demolishing a huge plate of ham sandwiches washed down with some fine wine recommended by Ronnie Moore when the name of Poole's Bill Holden was mentioned. Almost at once we were joined at our table by a smartly dressed character who asked in a thick American voice: 'One of youse guys want me?'

It didn't take more than a moment to realise we were in the company of one of the best stars of that era, William Holden. He stayed with us for quite a while, totally fascinated by what the pint-sized Peter had achieved in his cho-sen profession. When Peter asked him if he knew anything about speedway, the star said he had heard of the Milne brothers and Wilbur Lamoreaux but had never seen a race meeting. It was very late that evening when that particular SRA meeting broke up and we left the restaurant, and I don't know for sure who was most impressed – us seeing him, or him meeting Peter and the rest of the riders!

Peter took his role within the Association very seriously, and he received a lot of respect from his fellow riders. This was not only because he was a former World Champion, but also because he was very approachable and would go to great lengths to help out where he could. Furthermore, his position as Britain's number one rider meant that his opinion was greatly sought after – even if the officials didn't always like what they heard. Peter was a rider's rider, and he was well aware of the problems that both the novices and the established racers were faced with as the Sixties drew near.

After successfully defending the Britannia Shield and lifting the National Trophy, it was little wonder that Hoskins kept faith with the team that served him successfully in 1958. And with Peter Craven still only twenty-five years old, Belle Vue's boss could be forgiven for thinking that he had still to see the best from 'The Wizard of Balance'.

Peter was virtually unbeatable around his home track, and he was equally impressive on his travels. His overall league average was a whopping 11.00. The fact that he was still young and had yet to reach his peak seemed to suggest that when he did attain his personal level of excellence that every rider eventually finds in his career, it wouldn't be a question of when he would be beaten, but if.

Riders like Craven, Johnston, Fisher and Williams had all been together at Belle Vue for some time, and as a result they had all pro-gressed as racers, and developed as adults.

As we got more mature (older), Peter always, I felt, treated me like an older brother, said Williams. *He often talked to me about business – the greengro-*

cers business I had grown up in. I don't think Peter knew anything at all about it. It was certainly a passing interest, where we respected each other.

As the team travelled around the country to visit other tracks they would often travel in a convoy together. Even during the late Fifties, the Aces still enjoyed the support from loyal fans, and these supporters became known to the riders through Supporter's Club social events as well as meeting them at the race track. One such person in particular sprang to the mind of Peter Williams:

You will know that speedway has always had a percentage of fans who, while not being 100 per cent physically fit themselves, seemed to be attracted to Belle Vue and speedway, because it was a family sport; and you always felt safe – despite the crowds. Well there was a lady who had a calliper on her leg, who always brought her young son. He was maybe ten years old, and she brought him to all the meetings at Belle Vue. She was well known, but we never saw a father with them. Anyway, we often travelled in a sort of convoy to away meetings, and this time we were going to Norwich.

The cars stopped at a remote petrol filling station, which was miles from anywhere, and in that part of the world in the Fifties it was very quiet. As I got out to put petrol in the car, I walked round the back of the car and there was this lady and her son. Now this petrol station was so remote it was like landing on the moon, and yet these people were already there! I was absolutely flabbergasted – I just couldn't believe my eyes! I remember saying, 'What the hell are you doing here?' This was a filling station that was miles from anywhere with just a little hut and a few pumps. 'Oh, we are with Peter,' she said. I looked up and PC had stopped to fill up as well. Fisher and Johnno had stopped too. Peter was taking them, I think, to Yarmouth for a week's holiday, and he had arranged to meet them down that part of the country the next week so he could pick them up and bring them back to Manchester. I think they would have been in the Jupiter car. This act of care and kindness was typical of Peter. To me he was a boy, who never got spoilt by fame, who I would say was a great credit to his parents. We all have friends in our lives, but I count myself very fortunate to have known him as a friend and a team-mate.

Peter was in brilliant form during the opening months of the new season in 1959. As the holders, Belle Vue was the team to beat in the Britannia Shield competition. In fact, Peter was *the* rider to beat but very few could better him in the Northern Section. Admittedly the Southern Section was a tougher section than the one Belle Vue was in – their opponents were Coventry, Leicester and Oxford. Nonetheless, you couldn't take anything away from 'The Wizard of Balance'.

He raced unbeaten by a member of the opposition in all six qualifying matches in the Britannia Shield, and scored 88 points plus 2 bonus points for a perfect score. Surprisingly he was passed over in favour of his great rival, Ove Fundin, as the season's first challenger for Brian Crutcher in the Golden Helmet British Match Race Championship. Instead he faced Ron How in an eliminator race to earn the right to challenge the winner of the Crutcher *v.* Fundin clash. But this didn't please Johnnie Hoskins, who protested: 'He's England's greatest rider. His nomination should have been automatic.'

At one stage, the Aces were performing so well that some critics complained that the Manchester team was too strong and they should be forced to release either Dick Fisher or the New Zealander, Bob Duckworth. But in a cruel twist of fate, the Aces' season was dealt a huge blow from which they never recovered when Fisher crashed in May and broke his left leg.

Having already qualified for the Britannia Shield Final for the third successive year, they were expected to win the trophy again. They met Wimbledon in the final, but Fisher's injury came just two days before the first leg at Plough Lane. Despite the fact that the Dons were without both Ron How and Barry Briggs, they walloped them 59-31. Not even another maximum from Craven could prevent the London club from taking a massive lead to Belle Vue for the second leg. How had returned for the second leg, and they won there too by a score-line of 56-34. This defeat not only ended the Aces' stranglehold on the shield, but it also signalled a change of fortunes for the Northern giants.

They were also the holders of the National Trophy too, but they were knocked out of the competition at the semi-final stage by

Wimbledon – who went on to defeat Southampton to win the trophy. It was a memorable season for the new glamour club of London, as they completed a treble when they also retained the league championship. In contrast Belle Vue finished bottom of the league for the first time in their illustrious history, with only Craven and Johnston consistently performing at the level required for the National League.

Speedway Star & News writer, Danny Carter, was impressed with Peter's performances as he revealed that he was the first rider in the league to reach 100 points that season. PC won a list of individual meetings that year: Champion of Champs at Poole, the Champagne Derby and the Northern Cup at Belle Vue, International Derby at Ipswich, Pride of the East and the CTS Trophy at Norwich, and the Pride of the Midlands at Leicester. Carter wrote of his success in his weekly column:

I'm glad I'm not a promoter, or a man who puts up prizes or cups. 'Cos if I was, I'd be driven barmy by the sight of a confident, tiny, young perky-faced man presenting himself to collect them. The gent? Peter Craven, who else? Every time they put a cup up to be won at Belle Vue, they practically engrave his name on it – before the meeting even starts! He doesn't do so bad with records and trophies away from his own heap either.

Meanwhile, Johnnie Hoskins had re-opened New Cross and staged half a dozen open meetings there. No doubt he was mindful of the behind-the-scenes moves to introduce a new Second Division in 1960, as he brought Peter Craven, Ronnie Moore and other top stars to the venue to re-ignite interest in the sport which had not been staged there since 1953. Peter raced at this venue on the re-opening night for the Rangers team in a challenge match against Wimbledon. In front of 10,000 fans New Cross won 47-43. Speaking of the track, he cheekily said of the large hole he found while exiting the first bend: 'It's just like the Mersey Tunnel. You vanish down it and by the time you come up the other side you've lost half a lap.'

It was during another appearance at the New Cross track that his astonishing natural ability shone brightly, and confirmed that here was a man who had a gift from the gods when it came to racing a speedway bike. If the sport could be considered an art form, then surely it would be Craven that the students would study for inspiration.

This time he was riding for his beloved Aces when he seemed to 'disappear' from his machine on the back straight in heat 3. He vaulted back into the saddle with all the skill and confidence of a stunt-horse rider from an American Wild West show, and went on to win the race over Cyril Roger by several lengths!

The big individual meeting to be staged there was the Tom Farndon Memorial Trophy. Farndon was killed at the New Cross track in 1935, and a top-class field was assembled that included Craven, Briggs, Ronnie Moore, Peter Moore, Ron How, Nigel Boocock and Mike Broadbanks. But there was no stopping little Pete who won the meeting with an unbeaten 15-point maximum with a performance that left Ronnie Moore looking on in awe at the talent of the man. He said in his column:

One day I'll run a poll among the boys to see who they reckon is the cheekiest rider around the tracks. Until I do – and prove it – I'll just have to unofficially nominate my cheekie-chappie-champion – as Peter Craven. I guess he's got to speak up for himself. Being a bit on the small size (Pete says he carries around a built-in hole to stand in) we'd never know he was there otherwise. But the night he nipped round the New Cross track rather fastish and picked up the Tom Farndon Trophy – that was the limit. The story went around the pits that none of us need bother that night because it was Peter's pot. He had to win it as he'd just bought a larger cabinet to keep all of his trophies in. This was before the meeting had started. Then he went out and did the lot of us!

During a season when he seemed to sweep all before him, he was once again expected to be one of the favourites for the World Championship. He qualified safely for the Final at Wembley by winning the semi-final at Norwich – Fundin's home track – with another 15-point maximum. This gave him a combined total of 26 points, but so impressive was his form in 1959 that when he scored 11 points in the first of his semi-finals, many people thought that his form had finally begun to slip.

However, no rider can continue such fantastic form throughout the season without one off-night a year, and Craven's came at the worst possible time – the World Final. His bid for World Championship glory was over as early as heat 2, when he was left floundering at the back. Usually his silky passing skills would ensure that he soon left behind the unfamiliar surroundings of fourth place, but his attempt to round Ron How ended with a face full of shale. In his second race he was also a spectator, and he made hard work of passing Cyril Roger on the line for 1 point. He added 6 points from his remaining three rides to finish his sixth World Final with 7 points and was down in eighth place.

He hadn't made the best of preparations for the World Final when, as the pre-meeting favourite, he arrived late as he thought that the start time was 7.45 p.m. like it had been in the past – instead it was 7.30 p.m. A fellow World Finalist from Poland, Mieczyslaw Polukard – who scored 5 points – told journalists that he hoped that Peter would win the title. He went on to reveal how popular Craven was in Poland following his impressive performances there.

'I hope Peter wins tonight. All the Polish children have tiny Peter as their sporting idol,' he revealed.

Ronnie Moore won his second World Championship with a maximum that night, while PC seemed very relaxed and soaked up the atmosphere. It was reported that in between his races he spent his time sat on the wall signing autographs. And when he had scored just 1 point from two rides, he said: 'Well, I've got my easy ones over first. Now anything can happen,' he laughed. 'But next time I reach Wembley say that I haven't got a cat in hell's chance, the better I go,' he added with a cheeky smile.

Shortly before the World Final, Peter had to give up his post as a part of the Speedway Riders' Association because, although he was still eager to help in Association matters, his riding commitments were not allowing him to fulfil his obligations to his satisfaction. Reg Trott replaced the Belle Vue star, but the Association paid tribute to his 'wise counsel'.

Peter continued to help the SRA as his opinions were much sought-after as he was England's best rider. Later, when Cyril Hart had to resign from his role as the Secretary of the Association, he was another person who was impressed by not only Peter's willingness to go out of his way to help, but that he also remained untouched by the fame he enjoyed, as he recalled in this short article:

As a result of a career change I had only very recently, and of necessity, made a move from London to the Land of Green Ginger, the North Eastern sea port of Hull. I had no alternative but to offer my resignation as the Secretary of the SRA, and so quickly was the transition that the Association's furniture (filing cabinet, printing machine and paperwork) went up to Hull as well.

Clearly something had to be done, and Chairman Cyril Brine, in his usual helpful manner, said 'leave it to me'. So it was that the next thing that happened was a telephone call from his Liverpool home from World Champion Peter Craven to say that he was arriving on Wednesday afternoon to collect all the gear. Peter had responded to Cyril's request, and kindly agreed to drive across the country to collect the complete SRA office equipment for me. That was when my wife, knowing it would take quite a while to load up all the stuff, posed the question: 'What do you give a World Champion for tea?'

The loading complete, I nervously asked the lad if he would like to stay for tea with us, and while I felt so privileged when he thanked me and said he would love to, I admit to being worried about what to offer him. Chancing it, I made a poor joke of it saying we had no caviar in the fridge, that we had the last of the prawns yesterday, and that being a Wednesday the shops were shut.

Imagine my relief, to say nothing of my appreciation of Peter as a right down-to-earth character – and a Scouser at that! –when he replied simply: 'It would be lovely to have some bread and butter and jam, and a cuppa, with you both. I'd really like that.' I don't think my wife and I, either, have ever enjoyed a very plain tea time as much as we did the day the World Champion visited our home.

As a rider Peter had an uncanny ability to not only remain on the bike, defying gravity itself, and to have full control of it, but to be able to manoeuvre himself into positions from which he couldn't be challenged. In truth, on the track, at speed, he was unique.

Peter won his eliminator against Ron How to be able to challenge Fundin for the Golden Helmet, but he lost to the Swede. However, he had another opportunity to challenge him for the coveted title when he defeated Ronnie Moore in an eliminator race at Oxford on 31 July. He lost the first leg 2-1 at Norwich, but then forced a decider which he won 2-1 at Belle Vue.

The deciding leg was scheduled to be staged at Oxford, and Craven must have fancied his chances as he seemed to perform well around Cowley. However, the holder was unable to defend the match race title as the Swedish Federation refused to release him from his Swedish engagements, and he lost the title to the British number one by default. In fact, the Swedish Federation ordered their top rider to rest as he was due to race in the Swedish Championship in two days' time.

Therefore, to replace the much anticipated Match Race Championship, the Oxford promotion decided to put forward three challengers for Craven from a star-studded field that was assembled for a best pairs event. First of all he met Briggs, then Arne Pander, and then Ronnie Moore – he defeated them all. He then finished runner-up in the pairs with Oxford's Howdy Byford (Peter 12 Byford 6) with 18 points, losing to the Briggs/Roy Bowers pairing by 1 point.

Speaking of the Golden Helmet controversy, Craven told the press:

Last year I lost my chance of the title at the discussion table and not on the track. This year the boot is on the other foot. That's evened it out, I suppose, but I don't like it. I don't like winning anything this way. I reckoned I would have beaten Ove at Oxford anyway. He didn't agree, but we'd have settled it racing. That's the way it should be done, but if the title is given to me then that takes care of that.

What I find disappointing is that the Oxford spectators, through no fault of their own, have lost the chance of seeing the decider. I don't think they've had one before…now they haven't had one again!

With the exception of the World Final, Peter had another brilliant season. In a remarkable year for the Aces, only once did he fail to top the score chart. He also led England to a 2-1 Test series victory over Australasia which included 16 points in the Second Test at Norwich. *Speedway Star's* Eric Linden described him as fantastic and wrote of him: 'Wherever a man could lead, Peter led. Except that one important meeting, the World Championship, when he had a rare off night.'

Five

PETER THE GREAT

Australia is the nation where the sport is credited as originating from. It is also the country that provided the first World Champion, Lionel Van Praag in 1936, one of the most popular winners ever in Bluey Wilkinson in 1938, and they also provided the first back-to-back champion in Jack Young. Therefore, with some justification, it could be said that the country has provided some of the sport's greatest riders. But during the 1959/60 season, Oz would get the opportunity to see arguably Britain's best ever rider, as 'The Wizard of Balance', Peter Craven, was bringing his Atom show down under.

Nowadays, 'wintering' down under during Europe's close of season is no big deal. Modern air travel has made the world a smaller place, but in 1959 Peter admitted that he was experiencing some difficulty in finding a ship that would take his whole family to Australia.

Following his success racing in Europe, journalist Mike Kent described him as 'England's best ambassador'. He went on:

Craven is the nearest thing in modern-day speedway comparable with the old leg trailers of by-gone days. Spectacle, and that alone, typifies him on the track. In fact, wherever there has been top-class international racing and Craven has appeared, he has by virtue of his sportsmanship done more than any ambassador could to uphold the prestige of England.

Peter became the innocent victim of an administrative error when he discovered that he was expected to ride for England in a Test against Australia. He had agreed to ride at Rowley Park, Adelaide, and was contracted to ride at the venue by promoter Kym Bonython. The confusion seemed to have arisen when Peter had told Ken McKinlay that he would appear for his country if the matches did not clash with Mr Bonython's plans.

Naturally, Peter felt an obligation to the Australian promoter, because not only had he engaged his crowd-drawing skills, but he had also made arrangements for Brenda and his son to join him in the sun-kissed country. The First Test was scheduled for Rowley Park, but when the British Control Board discovered that Peter was not included in the touring party, they threatened to pull the plug on the Test's official status if he didn't appear. Furthermore, they released a statement saying that the Belle Vue Ace would be required to ride where the English team rides – against State Solo teams too.

Speaking in the Australian magazine, *Speedway Star*, Craven explained:

I hope it can be cleared up. I agreed to come out for the season at Rowley Park before the visiting team was chosen. Then Ken McKinlay asked me would I ride for England out here. I said I'd be here, and that I would ride where Mr Bonython's plans would not be upset. I've accepted an offer to ride for the season at Rowley Park, and I'll be riding at Rowley Park.

The Australians were impressed by Craven's friendly nature, and *Speedway Star* found his attitude particularly refreshing. 'Stop me when I've told you enough,' the magazine reported him as saying and enthused: 'Thanks a lot, Peter. We wish they were all so co-operative.'

The Test series went ahead without PC riding for them, and the First Test was switched from Adelaide to Melbourne. The English won all five of the matches with McKinlay leading the team – despite the fact that he was of Scottish nationality!

All the talk surrounding the arrival of England's former World Champion was the much anticipated clash with Australia's double World Champion, Jack Young. But when they met in the Solo State Championship it was the Aussie who won the meeting, as Peter struggled for power on the big circuit.

Peter had to do all of his own maintenance on his bikes while he was in Australia, said Brenda. *He always said that he wasn't mechanically-minded, but because he struggled early on, he stripped down his engines and found a few things that were not quite right. Once he rectified this he flew! And I think that proved a point. They did a lot of handicap racing out there, and the better you were the further back you had to start. Peter still won the races. They used to run other forms of racing during the evening, they used to have midget cars, sidecars, and bigger car racing (sedan racing) and it was a full night of entertainment that used to go on until midnight. They used to have the solo bike racing first. Then they used to have a barbecue afterwards. It was quite good fun. We were based at Adelaide and we used to see a lot of boys out there like Jack Young, and Aub Lawson. Peter coped all right with the heat, but there were times when he couldn't sleep at night because he was too hot. I didn't mind the heat at all, but Peter wasn't that keen on it.*

Ivan Crozier, who raced with Brian Craven in the Newcastle team, recalled in an article that appeared in the *Vintage Speedway Magazine* that Bob Tattersall's wife Dee was particularly smitten with Peter. During one of those great Aussie traditions, a barbecue, Robert was entertaining everyone as he sped around on his tricycle while his dad was equally popular with his sense of humour. Crozier wrote:

Dee couldn't keep her hands off Peter, and every time he approached the barbecue for a chop or a sausage, she'd goose him! Bob was laughing so much he fell over. His comedy timing was superb. I don't think he showed his back to her all night. It was an all night running comedy act. He even backed into his car when he was leaving.

Crozier was planning his first trip to race in England, and he was eager to learn as much as he could before departing. But Peter wouldn't open up to him at all — it sometimes pays to keep your cards close to chest while you are racing.

Peter's duels with Young and McKinlay caught the headlines down under. But it was a victory over Sweden's Kai Forsberg that seemed to put the English rider on the right road for success. He recovered from a 70-yard handicap to pass the field and win the handicap part of the programme finishing ahead of Jack Scott and Geoff Mudge.

By the time it was announced that he was due to face Jack Young in a special match race, he was displaying the sort of form that made him the talk of British speedway. Young was perhaps the only rider from the local brigade who could seriously threaten Peter now that he had adjusted to the environment, and had the track dialled in. In their first encounter they swapped the lead three times before Craven took control at the front and won the race.

While racing in Oz, the locals dubbed the popular Englishman 'The Flea', and most of the races were over three laps instead of the traditional four. This was because the track at Rowley Park was a lot bigger than the ones they race on in Europe, and it was used for car racing as well as bikes.

Peter also made an appearance at Claremont where he thrilled the crowds with some spectacular cornering to win the Stars Scratch Race from Dave Hankins and Nick Nicholls. Then he also won the International Stars Race, which featured a rolling start instead of the traditional standing clutch start. The following week he won the Golden Helmet at Claremont with an average speed of 60mph, and completed a Grand Slam of victories that night by winning the Stars Scratch Race and also the Bernie Dunne Handicap.

As Peter was underlining his reputation down under as one of the world's most spectacular and entertaining riders, the sport in Britain was undergoing a shake-up. Mike Parker and Reg Fearman inspired the launch of a new lower division called the Provincial League. It was run at reduced costs, and this enabled clubs like Liverpool, Rayleigh, Bristol, Cradley Heath and Sheffield to re-enter league competition. The new league included ten teams in total, and despite the lower standards that were on display, it captured the public's interest.

Internationally the World Team Cup was also launched for the first time in 1960, and its introduction was inspired by the enthusiasm of the Polish motor sports magazine, *Motor.* There was some debate about whether England would participate as themselves or as Great Britain – this was because they could then use the Commonwealth as a source of riders such as Briggs and Moore. This would eventually come to pass, but not yet . . .

However, while the above may not have affected Peter directly, the change at Belle Vue most certainly did. Ken Sharples took over from Johnnie Hoskins as the new promoter at the Zoo. Hoskins had decided to transfer all his efforts in reviving New Cross who he had taken into the National League. Peter Williams had decided to retire, and despite similar announcements from both Dick Fisher and Johnston, they both returned to join regulars Craven and Duckworth. However, Sharples launched a search for some new foreign talent and eventually signed Swede Gote Nordin.

Peter faced a determined Ronnie Moore as his first challenger for the Golden Helmet. Moore had gone on record to say that he wanted to win the title and hold on to it throughout the season. Pete made sure that the match race went to a decider at Oxford, and, given his well-known form around Cowley, he was expected to win. But on this occasion Moore defeated 'The Mighty Atom' with two straight wins to relieve the Belle Vue number one of the Helmet.

Despite this setback, Peter had begun his season in his usual form that included a victory in the season opener at Wimbledon, the Metropolitan Cup – he defeated Ron How in a run-off for the title. It appeared that he had brought his winning habit back with him from Australia. Belle Vue were also running high at the top of the Northern Section of the Britannia Shield and qualified for the Final where they met Wimbledon.

The Dons were once again looking like possible league champions, but the Aces won the first leg 56–34, and lost by a narrow score-line of 46–44 at Plough Lane to win the tie on aggregate 100–80. It was the third time in four years that Belle Vue had won the Britannia Shield, and their prospects were encouraging as they went about collecting more silverware.

Unhappily, things did not look so good for Peter's brother Brian. He had decided to make a track return with Liverpool in the newly-formed Provincial League, when he crashed heavily and broke his ankle. He had been performing extremely well for his home town club when he sustained the injury. Peter said of Brian's misfortune:

I knew it couldn't last. There was our kid going like a bomb at Liverpool. In fact you could almost say that the way he was riding he was Liverpool. So I told him things were going too well, and five minutes later he gets carried off the track on a stretcher. How lousy can your luck get, after all the lousy luck he's already had?

Tragedy hit the Belle Vue team when they travelled to Norwich in a National Trophy semi-final clash. Derek Maynard was killed in heat 14 of the match. Known as 'Tink', he struck a fallen rider's machine and was hurled into the safety fence, and split his crash helmet into two pieces. He was rushed to hospital but, sadly, succumbed to his injuries and died the following day.

Nonetheless, Peter put in some remarkable performances at international and world level throughout the 1960 season. It all commenced with the qualifying rounds for the new World Cup.

The tournament was run on a four-team basis, and the teams consisted of four riders and one reserve. Each team would be represented in each race by one member of their team, while they could use their reserve to replace a rider at any time during the match. England faced Australia, New Zealand and a team called 'The Challengers'. The latter was a team made up of riders from the three countries that were not selected for either England, Australia or New Zealand, and were racing for the right to get into the main team. What sense did it make to have a rider having to try his level best to beat his fellow countryman, and perhaps taking points off them that could cause them to lose the match, in order that he could get into the national team?

The team who had scored the most points over four legs would then qualify for the Final in Sweden, where they would meet teams from Scandinavia and Central and Eastern Europe. England's first round was at Wimbledon and they won with 35 points, 7 clear of second-placed New Zealand on 28. Peter scored a 12-point maximum, and then repeated his unbeaten run with another full house in the second round at Oxford – which England also won. Peter then equalled the track record twice at Swindon in the third round as he raced to his third maximum before dropping his first point at, of all places, Belle Vue. England were comfortable qualifiers for the Final as they won all of their rounds.

The best race that I ever saw Peter in was at Swindon in that World Team Cup round, said Leon Leat. *From the tapes he got in front, but he stalled in mid-corner, because he had forgotten to turn the fuel taps on! He sort of bent down, got the bike going and took off after the other three riders. He passed them and won the race and equalled the track record! That was quite brilliant, his ability really showed there.*

Qualification for the World Championship also saw Craven in fantastic form as he won both his rounds at Belle Vue and Ipswich with an unbeaten score at each circuit. This form continued in the semi-finals at Wimbledon and Norwich where he again won both meetings with 15-point maximums, and qualified for Wembley with an unbeaten total of 30 points – a clear 2 points ahead of his nearest challengers Ron How and Ken McKinlay. Prior to the Final he won the Pride of the Midlands tournament with another full house, and then scored another maximum as Belle Vue defeated Ipswich 61-29. Needless to say he was England's best hope of winning the World title, and most pundits believed that he was likely to finish inside the top three.

Prior to the World Final, Peter led England into their first World Team Cup Final at Gothenburg, Sweden. He top-scored with 8 points, but England could only finish in second place behind the hosts Sweden, who won every race except two. Surprisingly, Peter failed to register a race win – England's winners were McKinlay and How.

Among the team that evening was George White, who recalled one particular occasion he shared with Peter during their trips to race in Scandinavia.

After the World Final the line-up went to Oslo to do another meeting there. It was like a re-run, or replica final. I remember after the match we were on the ferry waiting to leave in the estuary. The boat was bobbing up and down and swaying, as we were having a meal. I remember it quite well because we had roast reindeer. Suddenly Peter turned to me and excused himself. He had gone very pale, and he went to the cabin we shared. I stayed a little while and got some fresh air, and when I came back all the Norwegians and what have you were drinking lager and I thought, 'oh no, I can't do that' and decided to go to our cabin. When I got there, I saw Peter asleep on the bed with all these cups, bowls and other things around him in preparation in case he was sick!

Peter was drawn at number 7 for his seventh World Final appearance, and actually arrived at Wembley as an unbeaten rider in the World Championship. He had ridden through twenty races and had yet to drop a point.

In his first race at Wembley he met Barry Briggs, Aub Lawson and Josef Hofmeister in heat 2, and started from grid 2. As the tapes rose it was Lawson who made an excellent start, but as the field roared into the first bend Craven was at the back – but not for long. He made a terrific recovery and emerged from the second bend in front, and he went on to win his first race with 20 lengths to spare over Briggs. It appeared that PC meant business as he raced around Wembley in the fastest time of the evening, 68.8 seconds.

There was no stopping the popular English rider in his second race either as he held a huge lead over Australia's Peter Moore and Poland's Marian Kaiser. But the 70,000-strong crowd gave a collective gasp as PC almost fell off on the last bend, but a slight body wiggle was all that was required to correct his slide and he had won his second race. He registered another easy victory in heat 12 as he defeated his Belle Vue colleague, Ron Johnston and former champion, Jack Young.

After all the riders had completed three rides, only Craven and the defending champion, Ronnie Moore remained unbeaten on 9 points. Ove Fundin was close behind on 8 – dropping his only point to Moore in heat 10. The battle of the leaders followed immediately after the third round of races had been completed. Craven faced Moore in heat 13, and he was on the inside gate with the Kiwi alongside him in gate two. Chum Taylor and Poland's Stefan Kwoczala made up the rest of the field. Craven made a super start and led down the back straight, with Moore in hot pursuit. The latter tried to sweep round the outside of his English rival, but he was held off. As the race settled down, PC kept a bike's length between them, but as he exited the final bend he gave a cautious glance over his shoulder. He took the chequered flag for another 3 points and the crowd stood and erupted into a chorus of cheers.

Peter was well placed to win his second World Championship as he had won his four races for a maximum of 12 points; this meant that his rivals had it all to do. However, he would have to wait an agonising four races before he could have the opportunity to clinch the title. He was scheduled to meet Fundin in heat 18, and the Swede had also won his fourth race, so this meant that Craven had to win their encounter to be crowned World Champion. If Fundin won with Peter in second, then a run-off would be required to determine the destiny of the 1960 World title – this was the decider. Furthermore, if PC was successful, then he would establish a unique record of riding through the World Championship as an undefeated rider.

Fundin started from gate two with Craven alongside him in grid three. The fast-starting Swede took the lead from the gate with Peter giving chase. As one lap was completed Fundin held a two-length lead, but Craven slowly began closing the gap. On the back straight of the final lap there was less than a length between them as they roared into the third bend. But just as the little Englishman appeared to be lining up a pass, he hit a hole on the track and was thrown forward onto his handlebars. Miraculously he managed to hold on and he retained his balance, but Fundin had gone.

Craven heroically sped over the finishing line in second place, but he was in obvious pain as he cruised back to the pits, with one hand on the throttle and the other clutching his injured stomach. He was helped off his bike when he arrived in the pits, and he slumped over in pain. He had finished the night with 14 points, but two races would pass before he was due to meet Fundin in a run-off for the championship.

Defending champion Moore won his last race to also finish with 14 points and a three-man run-off was required to find the 1960 World Champion. The question in the pits, though, was whether Peter would be fit enough to take his place in the race? Fit or not, he was not about to pass up the opportunity, and he began making his preparations. Bravely he took up the inside berth with Fundin alongside him and Moore off the outside.

Fundin made a slick gate, and blocked a move from the inside from Craven, and then he moved over on the back straight to see off the challenge from Moore – the Kiwi was squeezed up against the fence so tightly that he skinned his knuckles on the fence! Their dual continued until the third lap when Fundin established his superiority; and this gave Craven the opportunity to challenge Moore for second with a lunge around the outside – but it was too late. Fundin had won his second World title, Moore finished second and Craven was an unlucky third.

PC had displayed some of his best form ever at Wembley, but how much did his injury in heat 18 affect his chances? It appeared that he could well have won his last race if he hadn't hit that hole in the track, and he would have surely have clinched the title as an undefeated World Champion. Furthermore, it is doubtful that he had enough time to regain some level of comfortable fitness for the run-off within the time that elapsed between heat 18 and the run-off. At most it would have been ten minutes – was that enough? I don't think so.

He was not the sort of man to dwell on these things, that's speedway as the old saying goes, but as he stepped up to receive his bronze medal from the famous film actor of the time, Norman Wisdom, he must have wondered how the World Championship had slipped from his grasp. After all, the post-war finals at that point had indicated that 14 points was usually enough to win. Peter and Wisdom seemed to hit it off straightaway as they were observed fooling around trying to prove which one of them was the biggest. Norman won by a hair's breadth. They conversed with each other for quite some time after the presentations were over, but the next time they would meet at Wembley, the circumstances would be a bit different. Peter joked,

No excuses but after my wallop in the 18th heat, I felt that I was dying. I felt like a new man after 10 minutes though. Trouble was the new man wasn't as good as the one who'd been riding all evening! Still, I'm going to spray my bronze medal when I get home and swear you blokes have the score wrong,

In the six-match Test series against Australasia, Peter scored an 18-point maximum in England's draw at Norwich in the Second Test although England failed to win a single match in the series. However, later in the season the team travelled to Poland for a three-match series, which saw Peter produce one of the most dynamic and heroic performances ever seen by a rider wearing an England race-jacket.

Poland had improved a great deal since England last toured there in 1958, and they defeated England 2-1. Craven had already established a reputation behind the Iron Curtain as one of the best riders in the world, but no one could have predicted the kind of form that he displayed with such dominance.

England lost the First Test at Wroclaw 68-39, but skipper Craven registered an unbeaten 21-point maximum. He repeated the feat again at Rybnik for the Second Test – where England got closer losing 56-51. Then during the final Test at Leszno, he was instrumental in providing England with their First Test win when he shadowed team-mate Bob Andrews home in heat 17 for a match-winning 5-1 – and completed the senior Test series with a paid maximum which meant that he had not been beaten by a Polish international.

Before that series, England also took part in a secondary Test series against a Polish League side which finished as a draw. Peter scored an 18-point maximum at Nowa Huta, while he dropped his only point during the five-match tour to Marian Kaiser at Rzeszow which England lost 48-30 – Peter finished with 14 points.

It was a remarkable performance, and it is one which is still talked about today by the older Polish supporters. Even now Peter Craven is revered in the nation as the greatest British rider of all time. Incidentally, in Poland during that time, a slow handclap registered approval, while a series of prolonged whistles would greet the riders they disliked.

We had hundreds of letters from fans in Poland, said Brenda. *But unfortunately we couldn't read them because they were written in Polish! Peter was very, very popular over there.*

But Peter's international season wasn't quite over yet. He travelled to Vienna to participate in the Golden Helmet of Austria. Reigning champion and great rival, Ove Fundin, was among the field, with Ronnie Moore, Olle Nygren, Arne Pander, Barry Briggs, Ron Johnston and many more world-class stars. Denmark's Pander, who raced for Oxford, surprisingly never qualified for a World Final, but it wasn't because he didn't have the ability as he illustrated when he won the Austrian Golden Helmet with a 15–point maximum. Craven took second with 14, and Moore was third with 12. However, Craven's victory over Fundin in heat 19 brought the crowd to their feet, as Leon Leat explained.

Peter was racing very well and around this track there was grass before the spectators. Well, he was fending Fundin off and he put the Swede on the grass. The crowd went nuts, and when Peter returned to the pits he said: 'The crowd were cheering a lot in that race,' and I replied: 'They weren't cheering you, they were booing you, because you put Fundin on the grass!' I remember when we went to Austria they had a woman in the pits because she was one of the meeting organisers there. It was a big deal in those days to see a woman in the pits. Now of course there are as many women in the pits as there are men, but back then it was quite unusual.

Peter's European tour ended on a winning note, when he teamed up with Pander to win the International Pairs with 23 points (Craven 12

Pander 11) at Graz. Their superior team-riding skills saw off the challenge from the Swedish duo of Fundin and Nygren who finished with 21 points (Fundin 15 Nygren 6).

It had been another successful season for the Belle Vue flier and he finished with a league average of 10.75. Belle Vue improved dramatically on their previous year's performance to finish second behind champions Wimbledon. Peter was eager to see the back of the wooden spoon for finishing bottom in 1959, and he told one of the sport's journalists that a special ceremony should be staged to pass it on to the sport's biggest stirrer. But he wouldn't be drawn on who he thought that was.

On the eve of the 1961 season, Peter and Brenda celebrated the birth of their second child, Julie. It has been said by many people, including Ove Fundin, that Peter's daughter has grown up to be the spitting image of her father – in his ways and looks.

Towards the end of the 1960 season, Peter also made two appearances in a team representing Europe in a Test series against the in-form Swedish team. The Scandinavian giants comfortably won all three tests, and Peter raced in the first and third matches. He mustered just 3 points at Linkopping, but significantly top-scored for Europe at Malmo with 13 points.

I say significantly because that was the venue chosen for the first World Individual Final to be staged outside of Britain in 1961. Fundin's success had been enough to convince the FIM (the sport's world governing body) that Sweden should stage the 1961 Final. It was an historic decision, and represented the first signs that the power base was beginning to shift away from Britain. Soon Poland would also make a successful request to stage a World Championship final, but in 1961 it was announced that Wroclaw in Poland would hold the second World Team Cup final.

Peter once again won through his qualifying rounds with an unbeaten score to lead the qualifiers with 30 points – he won rounds at both Southampton and Belle Vue. He also qualified comfortably from the semi-finals finishing as runner-up in both rounds to Ron How at Southampton and Barry Briggs at Norwich, to finish with a total of 28 points. This put him through to the British Zone Final at Wembley, where the top nine qualified for the Final in Sweden.

The British Final – as it would soon be called – was staged at the Empire Stadium and it was obviously a meeting that was put together to make up for the loss of the World Final. A crowd of 50,000 watched the meeting in which most of the field rode under protest because of a faulty starting gate. As they were part of the Commonwealth, Australians and New Zealanders were also permitted to take part in the Final, and it was Barry Briggs who won the meeting with a 15-point maximum.

However, Peter was the innocent victim of the starting gate fiasco that saw the Ace receive boos and jeers from the crowd. The spectators had become frustrated by the different methods of starting that were employed such as the drop of a white flag, then a Union Jack flag, briefly the starting gate worked, and then it malfunctioned again, and then the races were started using the green light. The audience had already illustrated their displeasure by a slow handclap, but the situation became quite ludicrous when PC and Ronnie Moore rolled out for heat 19 level pegging on 11 points apiece.

Briggs had already clinched the title, so the result in heat 19 would determine the other podium places. Peter got a flying start before Moore, Jack Young and Nigel Boocock had even begun to move. Moore and the crowd expected a re-start; but it never came. The fans hissed, booed, jeered and slow handclapped as Peter took the chequered flag in first place. Never before, or since, had he been greeted by such derision from the crowd, and the jeering continued when Peter was taking his place in the presentations.

When it comes to winning the World Championship, all the riders put in a special effort. Some of them have a special engine that they keep especially for use in the sport's premier competition, and they are always on the lookout for something that may give them the edge over their rivals for the sport's big event.

The JAP machine was almost unopposed as the power plant of choice among the leading riders, but with the sport beginning to develop in Europe there were signs that a rival was emerging to challenge their dominance. The Eso – which meant 'Ace' - engine would eventually enjoy worldwide fame in speedway racing, and would become better known as Jawa. It was developed and manufactured in Czechoslovakia, and although it was based on the JAP conception, it was purpose built for the sport. It took less maintenance than its rival but, significantly, it was able to feed the power through more evenly, and this favoured the riders who preferred the full throttle-style of racing. Ove Fundin was the first rider of world-class standard to try the engine, but the Speedway Riders' Association feared that this new machine would increase the riders' costs, and so cause more financial worries for the sport.

Fundin was the rider who the factory hoped would give them the credibility that they needed on the world's stage to develop the bike. But as the Swede recalled, it was Peter Craven who stepped forward and explained to him that it wasn't the time to introduce new, more expensive technology.

He said, only a handful of us could afford to buy a new bike, and if we bought better equipment then we would have been even further ahead of the others and the racing wouldn't have been any good at all. It was a clever way of putting it, and we agreed that it wasn't the right time after our discussion. I honoured the agreement because I thought it was a good idea. He didn't try to scare me off or anything, he just asked me. I think he was very much a gentleman, a little bit like Aub Lawson used to be.

Fundin's decision not to pursue the Eso/Jawa project probably didn't go down too well with the factory's bosses, and in 1965 Barry Briggs took up the agreement. The Kiwi won the factory's first World Championship in 1966, and but for a solitary win for Fundin on a JAP in 1967, they dominated the world of speedway racing until Peter Collins won the title on a British Weslake in 1976. Jawa continue to be one of the sport's leading engines, and although they don't dominate the sport quite as much as they used to, the engine is still one of the sport's leading motors. If it hadn't been for the intervention of Craven, Jawa could well have wrestled control away from the JAP a lot earlier than they did.

The 1961 World Final in Sweden was also notable for the inclusion of the first Soviet Union rider to make the last sixteen, Igor Plechanov. It was another indication that the nations behind the Iron Curtain were emerging to challenge the West. But the night belonged to Sweden who made a clean sweep of the medals, with Fundin retaining his crown and his fellow countrymen, Bjorn Knutsson and Gote Nordin, filling the other medal positions.

25,000 fans watched the final, and it wasn't a good one for Peter, who fell in his opening race and handed a win to Fundin. England's top rider took a blow to his head during his opening ride. It did seem at one point that he may have to withdraw from the meeting, but he bravely continued and finished with 6 points that included a race win in his third outing. However, he once again played his role as Britain's unofficial speedway ambassador as he was seen conversing with Plechanov – with the help of an interpreter. He seemed to be doing his best to warm-up relations between the Eastern Bloc and the West, when after the meeting they exchanged body colours. Plechanov finished ahead of the Englishman when they met in heat 17, but he finished down the field with 4 points.

As the World Final was such a big occasion, Peter made arrangements for his family to make the trip to Sweden. Joan Craven recalls:

Six of us went to Malmo in a big car; it was a Zodiac or a Zephyr or something like that. There were Brian and me, Peter and Brenda, and Derek Skyner and his wife. It was a big occasion and it was a lovely time, but Peter had a crash in that meeting and picked up an injury, so he didn't do so well. But that was Peter's way – he would get us all involved like that because the family was so close and it still is. I think what I remember most about that period was that it was a wonderfully happy time. Brian and Peter were great family men, so it was a special time. There was an innocence about it all, as we were all together and we were very proud of Peter. He was dynamite on a speedway bike.

Peter went about his business in his usual manner, but by his very high standards he had a somewhat quiet season. He was again the top scorer for Belle Vue, and was second only to Southampton's Swedish sensation, Bjorn Knutsson, in the league's top scorers with 400 points.

Belle Vue's manager Ken Sharples regarded a clash between Craven and Fundin as the greatest race he had ever seen at Hyde Road. The Aces were expected to lose to Norwich but they pulled off a memorable win, but the on-track thrills supplied by the old rivals in heat 11 moved Sharples to declare that it was a duel that would stay long in the memory.

The fast-starting Fundin snatched an early lead with PC in hot pursuit. Three absorbing laps followed with Craven losing and then gaining ground as he battled to find a way by the silky smooth Swede. Then he swooped around the outside of Fundin on the pits bend in breathtaking style to cross the line in front.

'The roar that greeted this win – not only in the last few breathless seconds of the race but indeed practically the whole of it – had not been heard in the stadium for a long time,' reported Frank Maclean.

During the season the razor manufacturer Remington had decided to sponsor some individual tournaments at Provincial League tracks, and some second-half races in the National League. Peter was the recipient of one of these prizes, but as Ronnie Moore recalled, the cheeky Liverpudlian couldn't help but play a prank on the organisers.

He won a Remington razor in a scratch race final, took it out of the case, walked into the speedway office with an empty case and demanded to know: 'Hey is this the new lightweight model, or was I racing for the cardboard box?'

There was panic for a few minutes while Peter kept a straight face. Then when he had everybody convinced that he really didn't have the razor, he burst out laughing. There was never a dull moment when Peter was around.

During another second-half event at Southampton, he demonstrated to Leon Leat how easily he could raise his game when he had to.

We used to have second halves in those days, and they used to be sponsored and there was usually a prize for the winner, recalled Leat. *I remember that after I oiled and doped his bike, Peter said to me: 'You know I'm not too bothered about this race.' And I said to him, 'It's a nice clock, Brenda would like it.' 'Oh all right then,' he said. And he went out there and won it, and passed everyone from the back.*

Belle Vue finished third in the league championship, and Peter made an unsuccessful challenge to relieve Fundin of the Golden Helmet. But he captained England to their second World Team Cup Final appearance. Common sense had finally prevailed and the Challengers team was dropped. Instead England faced just Australia and New Zealand in the qualifying rounds. After successfully qualifying for the Final, England were only spectators to the battle for the top spot between Poland and Sweden which the Poles won by just 1 point. England was third with Peter finishing as their top scorer with 8 points – he won his third race.

Eager to keep the magic of the Test matches alive, the decision was taken to stage a Great Britain *v.* Sweden Test series that saw the Commonwealth riders included in the British side. Craven continued to lead from the front, despite the inclusion of stars like Briggs and Moore. He finished top of Great Britain's scores in both the five-match series in England and Sweden. England won the series at home 5-0, but the Swedes reversed the score during the return in Scandinavia.

This series was a precursor to Great Britain also taking part in the World Team Cup instead of England in 1962 – this was mainly due to the fact that Craven was the only genuine world-class star that was in the England team, although Ron How might have had something to say about that. But there was no denying that the inclusion of Briggs and Moore did make the British side a formidable proposition.

During the Third Test at Belle Vue, the Swedes included a young rider in their side who impressed the Aces' management with 9 points. His name was Soren Sjosten who joined Belle Vue in 1962 and went on to become one of the Aces' best riders. Sjosten's style of riding was similar to that of Craven, and some fans regarded them as being almost a mirror image of each other – although the Swede was slightly taller than Peter. Ronnie Moore was quoted as describing the spectacular Swede as a 'Peter Craven-sized bomb'. No doubt the Aces' decision to sign the Swede was encouraged by the success of Gote Nordin, but what transpired was that Belle Vue had the most spectacular spearhead in the National League – the like of which Belle Vue would not see again until the Peter Collins/Chris Morton spearhead in the Seventies and Eighties. Furthermore, Craven had gone out of his way to help Sjosten when he came to the UK for the Test series, so Soren was quite happy to sign for Belle Vue.

Sjosten's arrival at Hyde Road came when it became apparent that Ron Johnston had decided to retire, and Bob Duckworth was also ruled out through injury. Consequently, at one point, team manager Ken Sharples only had Craven, Dick Fisher and the promising Jack Kitchen as certain starters for the Aces. Gote Nordin and Rune Sormander were also ruled out because of restrictions placed on European riders at the request of the SRA during the winter – originally the decision was taken to ban all foreign riders that were not from the Commonwealth, but this rule was later reversed and a small number were allowed to compete in Britain. Sjosten made an immediate impression, and began to register some useful scores from the moment the tapes went up on his debut race for the Aces.

In 1962 Peter, Ove Fundin, Barry Briggs, Ronnie Moore and Bjorn Knutsson were all considered to be so far ahead of everyone else, that the British Speedway League decided that they should handicap the riders 20 yards to give the rest a chance. With the exception of Knutsson, whose night of glory was yet to come, the other riders had shared the World title between them during the last eight years – and would continue to battle it out over the next six years. Their stranglehold on world speedway was so tight that it would take an exceptional rider to break it – and this rider was Ivan Mauger who made the World title his own with three successive victories in 1968, 1969 and 1970.

Certainly in speedway there have never been five such talented riders to maintain their grip at the very top for so long and in such numbers. One would be hard pressed to find a similar situation in other forms of motor racing, and the closest any sport has come to replicating those circumstances in recent times was in the 500cc Grand Prix during the early 1990s, when Wayne Rainey, Eddie Lawson, Kevin Schwantz, Wayne Gardner and Mick Doohan were making their presence felt on each others back wheels around the world's road racing circuits. Therefore, these speedway riders were dubbed the 'Top Five' or the 'Big Five'. Whatever they were called as a collective group, there was no doubt that they were very special riders indeed.

The 'Top Five' were handicapped 20 yards from the start line in the British National League competition, and there were other riders of heat leader standard that were also handicapped 10 yards. It was a controversial decision to introduce this new system of starting, and it was another indication that British speedway was struggling to keep the fans interested.

John Hyam, writing in *Speedway Star & News*, commented, 'The general impression of the speedway public is that handicap racing is National League speedway's last chance to bring the public back through the turnstiles.'

As well as the above riders, internationals like Ron How, Nigel Boocock and Ken McKinlay were also handicapped 10 yards. However, during the opening weeks of the new season, there were some teething problems with an over-complicated system that led to a meeting being called by the Speedway Riders' Association.

There were grumbles coming from the riders over the pay structure, and also a system which was devised that saw the BSPA committee meet once a month to revise the handicaps. Basically, certain riders would receive a different start-line handicap for each track. It was reported that there were some tracks that were keen to stop the handicap system under its original rules, but they changed their minds once the new plans were put in place. It was the idea of Coventry's Charles Ochiltree that the star riders would continue to start from 20 yards back from the start line, with the exception being the riders appearing at number six and seven who would start from the conventional start line. The others would be handicapped 10 yards. Moreover, the riders were also given a pay increase which was said to be 'over 20 per cent'. One official was quoted at the time as saying, 'The promoters themselves are now enthusiastic that they have something to offer the public. With this spirit aboard, the time is ripe for a real speedway revival.'

Needless to say this system did throw up a few surprise race wins for the lesser lights, but by and large the 'Top Five' were not troubled too much by having to give at least a 10-yard advantage to their rivals. Due to some of the rider shortage problems that the Aces were faced with, they gave Jim Yacoby an opportunity to prove his ability. He was paired with Craven that season and he believed that the handicap system was not such a handicap at all.

When they had the handicaps, Peter would always be alongside in a flash. In fact I always thought that the handicaps actually helped them because they were able to gather more speed for the first turn, believed Yacoby. *I remember on one occasion, on the first turn he was on my outside, and when I looked across at him he pulled down his goggles and looked straight at me while he was in the middle of the turn! He didn't have his foot on the ground – he was riding on pure balance. The tracks were a lot deeper in those days and the bikes were harder to ride than they are now. With that balance of his he could get round the small tracks like Wimbledon and Oxford as well as big ones. As a rider myself, you appreciated how good he was – he was so talented.*

Following the retirement of Johnston, PC was made the captain of Belle Vue and he wasn't just a captain in name. He was always on hand to assist his team-mates, and along with Harold Jackson he would also help with mechanical issues too. But as Yacoby recalled, being Peter's partner on the track was a double-edged sword. On the one hand you had your captain to look out for you, but on the other you came up against the very best riders in the league – always.

I used to ride with Peter as his partner, and the problem was that you were always coming up against opponents like Fundin, Moore and Briggs, and this was hard for a rider like me to get in amongst the points. Peter would always help you with advice, and he was good like that – a great captain. And he would always look for you on the track, but he was so fast. But the thing was that I found it hard to keep up with him and he used to say: 'If you can't go any faster I shall have to leave you.'

Belle Vue struggled at the start of the season, as they missed the scores from their retired Kiwi duo of Johnston and Duckworth. The club looked to Peter to lead from the front, and with the extra pressure of the handicap system, it wasn't quite so easy to get maximums – but regular double-figure returns were no problem to him.

As well as PC, Sjosten and Yacoby, the side also included Dick Fisher, Jack Kitchen, Nick Nicholls, Peter Kelly and the also Bernard MacArthur. A series of defeats during the opening weeks of the season meant that Sharples had to strengthen his side. He signed Cyril Maidment from Wimbledon, and then later in the season Split Waterman also made a handful of appearances for the Manchester club.

The situation seemed to have been reversed when the Aces demolished the Ove Fundin-led Norwich team 51–27 at the end of May. It was another meeting that produced a classic race between the old rivals Craven and Fundin. PC had already beaten the Swede twice in two challenge match races before the contest between the two clubs, when they met again in the final race of the night.

Craven's team-mate, Dick Fisher was also in the race, while John Debbage was the Stars' other rider. Craven, Fundin and Fisher were shoulder to shoulder during the first lap. Fundin nosed in front, but the crowd roared with approval as the Aces duo took advantage of a slight drift wide by the Swede on the pits bend to lead. But the Swede had extra speed at his disposal from coming off the banked turn and regained the lead on the back straight. Craven put in a captain's effort and mounted another challenge, but Fundin held firm. Suddenly Fisher found some grip and caught Fundin and was able to slightly move the

Swede out toward the fence. That was just the opportunity that Craven needed and he seized it with both hands, racing inside the two riders to take the lead. Fundin, though, shrugged off Fisher and pressured his rival, Craven, for a grandstand finish with a strong challenge on the final bend. Shoulder to shoulder they raced to the chequered flag; every neck in stadium was straining for a view and Craven won by the inches on the line. Journalist Frank Maclean said of the race that it would be 'a talking point for many years to come in Manchester'.

Peter's style was about balance, said Yacoby. *He was so fast and he could ride any track. He could get traction where others couldn't. He was special and he knew how to ride. The only rider who bothered him, I believe, was Fundin. I think because he relied on his balance when he rode, I think he was worried that Fundin would dive underneath him. I think he felt a bit vulnerable when he raced against him.*

This concern over Fundin diving inside him could also be the reason behind Alan Morrey's view of the Craven-Fundin clashes. 'For some reason Peter was a little bit scared of Fundin. I don't know why because he was a fair rider, but he was a bit intimidated by him. He used to beat Fundin; I don't what it was, but he was definitely a little bit fazed. I think Fundin was the only rival that Peter was wary of.'

However, Belle Vue's first track action of that season was not in Britain but in Austria. They faced the local club, Austrian Motor Race Club, and the Swedish team, Kaparna, in a three-team contest. The Aces were represented by PC, Dick Fisher and Jack Kitchen, and were bolstered in the international-billed event by Bob Andrews and Arne Pander. Unfortunately the Aces finished a lowly third in the first match in Vienna, but Craven won the Golden Helmet by winning all of his three races against Pander, and the German Josef Hofmeister. The Aces then won the second match at Linz, and PC retained the Helmet with a faultless display. This situation continued for the third match, and Peter finished the short tour as the Austrian Golden Helmet champion as the Aces had won the series.

One of Peter's early season engagements was on a two-wheeled variety of a different kind. He was the president of the Wilmslow Hammers Cycle Speedway Team, and a special challenge match between the Hammers and the Speedway Riders from Belle Vue was arranged. It was staged in aid of the British Empire Cancer Campaign on 29 April, and the contest finished as a 48-48 draw.

However, Peter and Brian Craven both took part but failed to make much impression for the speedway team, with just Brian scoring a solitary point. Top scorer was Lou Crepp who scored 14 points, and he received solid backing from Bernard MacArthur (13) and Derek Skyner (12). David Blinston, who was present at the meeting, informed me that Crepp was the first British Cycle Speedway Champion, and that Skyner had told him that he had ridden the pedalled version before in Liverpool.

Ernie Hancock was now one of the *Speedway Star & News'* roaming journalists, and he would often meet Peter on his travels. But no matter how often he had seen him, Peter always greeted Ernie like he had not seen him for years.

I think Peter was the best rider of all time, and he was my favourite rider, admitted Hancock. *In my role as a speedway journalist I used to be in the pits with the riders and, of course, I knew a lot of them. But Peter was more of a friend, and when we used to meet he always asked after my well-being and would also ask where my mother was. He would go up to her and have a chat, and he would always give her kiss on the cheek. He was a charming man, and quite a happy-go-lucky character.*

Peter entered the World Team Cup as a member of the Great Britain team who were seeded direct to the final. They finished as runners-up to Sweden at Slany, Czechoslovakia, and Peter scored 6 points. It was his only international team engagement that year, and his preparation could not have been helped by a hectic schedule that saw him race in four meetings in four days that included the World Team Cup in Czechoslovakia.

Once again Britain's hopes of World Championship glory rested with the diminutive rider from Liverpool. There was no doubt that he was England's top rider, and this was underlined when he finished third in the Internationale at Wimbledon behind the winner Fundin and Barry Briggs. He was the only rider to defeat Briggs who lost a run-off to Fundin for overall victory. But Pete's third place appeared to suggest a start of a memorable season. The sport's pundits and the supporters began to sense that Craven was coming into some of the best form of his career.

As had happened the previous year, the qualifying rounds for the World Championship doubled-up as the British Championship. As usual Peter entered the World title chase in the second set of qualifying rounds and began at Oxford. He won that round with an unbeaten 15 points even though it rained throughout the meeting. Next he travelled to Leicester where he won again with 14 points – dropping his only point to Ron How. Finally he came home to Belle Vue where he predictably walked off with the winner's cheque with another unbeaten score – he had made light work of qualifying for the semifinals.

Vic White was riding for Leicester in the Provincial League, and he was one of the meeting reserves for the World Championship round. It seemed that Craven had become the yardstick from which all British riders must be judged.

I was having a good spell with Leicester in the PL, having broken the track record just a week or so earlier, White recalled. *I was first reserve and in one race someone pulled out, or broke the tapes and I got a ride (it was Cyril Brine who pulled out after suffering mechanical problems in his previous race). In this race, of course, were Peter, Teo Teodorowicz and Brian Brett. Needless to say Peter won the race and I came last, but my biding thought was that by the end of the meeting no rider had done a time as fast as my track record. This, of course, proved nothing, but it was nice to be able to say that none of the first division guys had gone as fast as I had – not even Peter.*

The semi-finals were scheduled to be held at Wimbledon, Southampton and Norwich. Held over three meetings, the top scorer on aggregate would be crowned British Champion. The top eight would qualify for the World Final at Wembley. There was extra interest in 1962 for the Craven family, as brother Brian had also made it to the semi-finals, and there was a possibility that he could also make it to the World Final. In spite of business interests, he had been enjoying his best season at Provincial League, Newcastle, and he eventually finished third in the Provincial League Riders' Championship – he won two qualifying rounds at Stoke and Middlesbrough to lead the qualifiers with 43 points.

Peter was in excellent form in the first meeting at Wimbledon as he won the event with 14 points – dropping his only point to Wimbledon's Ronnie Moore. Meanwhile, his brother Brian was finding that National League opposition was a lot tougher at this level, and he was left with a mountain to climb when he finished his night's work with just 4 points. The next day the sixteen riders moved to Southampton where once again Peter reigned supreme with another unbeaten score. Brian's hopes were over as he scored just 1 point. The final semi was at Norwich, and Peter led the scores with 29 points but his nearest challenger was defending champion Barry Briggs who had 26, while Moore was further behind on 24.

Briggs was in scintillating form, and he was unbeaten as he won the final round that put him on an aggregate total of 41 points. Craven finished with 12 points and also finished with 41. Therefore, a run–off was required to decide the 1962 British Champion.

However, Peter could rightly feel aggrieved that he was in this position as he was the innocent victim of an incident during the opening heat. In those days it was legal to touch the tapes, but the rider would be excluded if he broke them. After he had nudged the tape, the tape got caught up on this mudguard. But when he pulled back the referee released the tapes – leaving him and Nigel Boocock stranded at the start line. Craven and Boocock expected the referee to order a re-start – but he didn't. The other two riders, Moore and Ron How, had hesitantly carried on and this left the stranded riders to reluctantly follow suit, with PC managing third place. This meant that Peter was left chasing the title, when, instead, he could have been in a much stronger position.

Before they met in the run-off, Peter had already lost to Briggs. The Kiwi had won a thrilling heat 19 and had to come from the back to defeat the Belle Vue rider. In the run-off, however, it was Briggs who took an early lead, but Craven passed him and held on to win his first British Championship. The only downside to his triumph was the failure of his brother to make the final, but it was clear that he lacked experience at this level and he finished with just 7 points.

An incredulous Ronnie Moore was once again left to marvel at Craven's brilliance, and his knack of rising to the occasion in the World Championship. Peter had won two of the top cheques for £50, and also £40 for winning the British title. Then if you add the other three qualifying rounds which he also won, that was another £60. Moore suggested in his column in *Speedway Star & News* that he may have got carried away. He complained:

If Peter doesn't work for the Sunday Pictorial *[the sponsors] then he ought to. It would be cheaper for them to have him on the staff than have him running around loose, snapping up all their loose cheques. The rest of us were wasting our time trying to keep him away from them.*

I know Pete is buying a new house in Liverpool, but holy smoke, he doesn't have to pay for it all at once. It really is a fantastic record – six meetings, six cheques. Maybe when Wembley comes along Pete can bring his total up to seven? While every one of us is out to stop him, there would hardly be a more popular winner if he pulled it off.

Peter maintained his form for Belle Vue as the Aces moved up the table, but they were never championship contenders. However, Craven *was* a World Championship contender, and Moore was not the only one who thought that he could win the title. Shortly before the Final was staged, the eyes of the speedway world were focused on

Oxford for the 'Kings of Oxford' trophy. With the exception of the injured Fundin, it was almost a dress rehearsal for the night at Wembley as seven finalists were included in the field.

Craven was the defending champion, and he was in no mood to surrender the trophy. He and Bjorn Knutsson were unbeaten as they lined up for the final, the decider. Briggs was also in the race with Olle Nygren. Knutsson led the race until his chain snapped when he was just a few yards from the finishing line. Briggs, followed by Craven, sped by the unlucky Swedish international and the title remained in Craven's hands. There was no doubt that he was lucky to retain the 'Kings of Oxford' trophy, but so often fortune had not smiled on the likeable Liverpudlian and he was due a bit of luck. Could this have been an indication that Fortune was about to look favourably upon him, and was that long-awaited second World title going to be his at last?

Despite his encouraging form, most of the press seemed to be settling for a win for either Fundin or Briggs. No one discounted Craven's chances, but it seemed no one trusted Peter's luck – or lack of it. There was a lot of interest in the qualification of the Russian, Igor Plechanov, who would make history as the first Russian rider ever to race in England. Furthermore, he was no slow coach either, and he had the experience of riding in the 1961 Final under his belt, so he was expected to do better than he had done on his debut appearance.

Also making his second World Final appearance – although not on a bike – was film star Norman Wisdom. He had struck up a friendship with Peter at the 1960 final, and even if he didn't step up to collect a prize it was expected that they would have much to talk about. Ronnie Moore said in his column that Wisdom had planned to take over the community singing before the event to warm things up!

Briggs' chances of glory also took a setback when he was involved in a car accident in France that left him with a badly bruised eye after being hit by a stone. But it seemed that this would be a minor irritation as the big night arrived on 8 September 1962.

Peter wore the number fourteen race-jacket and began his bid for glory in gate two of heat 4. An unsatisfactory start was called following Rune Sormander's tumble after a tight first turn, which meant that Pete had to do it all again. This only added to the tension, but Peter was the last to emerge from the pits and calmly strolled over to his waiting machine while his rivals anxiously waited for the former champion. Sormander and Craven produced another competitive first bend, but it was the Swede who led as they roared into the third bend. Craven took to the outside on the fourth turn, and spectacularly broadsided his way past Sormander on the next turn and was never troubled as he bagged his first victory.

Ronnie Moore once said that everyone suffers from nerves during the World Final night except Peter Craven. 'He struts around same as always,' he observed, 'and tells you how much he is going to win by. Cocky is Pete; but it's the kind of cockiness that you don't link up with a big head.'

Heat 6 brought together the four leading riders: Briggs, Craven, Fundin and Knutsson. It was described as 'the big one'; and it was indeed a race that would have a huge bearing on the outcome of the final. It was a vital race for all of the four riders, but especially for Briggs who had scored just 1 point in his first ride, while the other three riders had won their opening races. Therefore, the New Zealander knew that he had to win this race to keep alive his hopes of glory.

Briggs made a lightening start, but behind him the other three riders were squabbling over the minor placing on the first bend. Fundin was pressured by Craven, and the Swede got tangled up with his fellow countryman Knutsson and he appeared to hit his back wheel. As they emerged onto the back straight, it was Fundin who was last, Knutsson was second with Craven in third. PC stormed around the outside of Knutsson on the third bend of the final lap, and he managed to get within a length of Briggs at the finishing line. The Kiwi's victory had thrown the championship wide open.

Moore had won heat 7 and he had won his first two rides to lead the pack. Therefore, when he met Craven in heat 11 it was another important race. But Craven raced into the lead, and never looked back. Unfortunately for Moore, his engine gave up and his championship hopes died with it. But after all the riders had completed three rides, it was PC who led the score chart with 8 points, Briggs and Ken McKinlay had 7, Moore 6. Knutsson's challenge had ended with an engine failure, while Fundin had just 4 points after a terrible third ride where he was caught up in a dice with Craven's Aces' colleague, Soren Sjosten.

Peter faced McKinlay in heat 13, but he burst around the strong Scotsman and won the race with a massive margin to reach 11 points. But in a strange scenario, Peter had to wait until heat 20 before he could make sure of the title. He watched nervously from the pits as he saw first Briggs, then Fundin and Knutsson win their third races. Subsequently, Fundin, Briggs and Knutsson again took the chequered flag to keep the pressure on the little Englishman as he prepared for his final race.

It was Briggs who was his main challenger as he had 13 points. Fundin had finished on 10, and couldn't catch Craven even if he finished last. Pete had to win his last race to clinch the championship. If he was second then he would face Briggs in a run-off; a third and the title was lost and he would finish in second.

Peter was in grid two, inside him was Poland's Pawel Waloszek, in grid three was the Russian Plechanov – who had one race win to his name – and on the outside was Sjosten. It had been seven years since England had last crowned a World Champion; seven years had passed since Peter had last won the World Championship; could this be the moment when he established himself as England's best-ever rider? Peter answered this question with an emphatic 'yes' by taking an easy win and he seemed to coast home as Sjosten and Plechanov argued over second and third behind him. Peter Craven had done it; he was the first – and only - Englishman to win the World Championship twice.

His success was greeted with a roar of appreciation from the 62,000-strong crowd, and he happily stepped up to renew his acquaintance with Norman Wisdom as the Champion of the World. Briggs was second, and Fundin defeated Knutsson to take third. The *Speedway Star & News'* headlines said, 'Cheeky Craven is champ' and went on: 'magnificent Peter using every bit of the track and showing the full thrill of the flat-out broadside time and again. He alone consistently made an impression from the back.'

A less than surprised Ronnie Moore, who finished with 9 points, said: 'Peter Craven was a very worthy winner. Congrats Pete, and may all your troubles be just worrying where to put the silverware you keep winning.'

Seven years may have passed since he won his first World title, but the press interest in his pyjamas was just as keen as it was then. It was revealed that he had changed them from a red and white pair to a blue and white pair.

'I have had a very good season and I'd thought I'd pension the other pair off,' said Peter. 'They started out as red and white but got washed so often the stripes had changed over to white and red.'

In 1955 he was looked upon as a surprise winner, because he had yet to really establish himself as a consistent world beater. But in 1962 there were no doubts about the worthiness of his victory: he was England's undisputed number one, he was also one of the 'Top Five', and he should have won the title at least once more before 1962. Peter Craven had now joined the select band of riders that have won the title more than once – an achievement that takes on more significance when one considers the strong competition he faced.

'He won because he was the hottest, fastest, smartest thing on two wheels that night,' wrote journalist Angus Kix. 'And you can say that about him for most nights of the season too.'

It seemed that the introduction of handicap racing had not taken the edge off his racing. 'I have never ridden better in my life than I have this season. The handicap has added to my racing. I now feel a much better rider than I did in 1955,' he said.

Peter was fully loaded as he left the pits with the spoils of victory. He was struggling along with the Winged Wheel World Championship trophy that was packed in a crate which was almost as big as the champion himself! But no doubt it was a burden he was happy to bear.

His unofficial role as Britain's speedway ambassador was in operation again during World Final night, when Igor Plechanov was particularly impressed by the hospitality that was shown to him by the World Champion. So much so in fact, that he was invited to Russia to race on the basis of the praise that the Russian rider heaped on his English rival when he returned home. Unfortunately, Peter was unable to accept their invitation because of his commitments in Britain.

However, the act of kindness he showed Plechanov did have a positive outcome for this developing speedway nation, because the Speedway Control Board invited a USSR team to tour the British tracks in 1963. Once again the personality of Craven had proved a hit with our Continental cousins, and his influence had been the catalyst for the sport's borders to be re-drawn. Soon the Soviet Union would develop – briefly – into one of the sport's major countries.

Peter received so many messages of congratulations from everyone that he told *Speedway Star & News* that he would have to take three months off to reply to them all. Unfortunately, he had to turn down a request to attend the annual FIM dinner in Brussels in order to be able to race in Belle Vue's final meeting of the season. He would have received his medal at the dinner, but the Aces came first.

Peter was unsuccessful in his attempt to relieve Ove Fundin of the Golden Helmet – this was despite being handed victory in the second leg at Belle Vue because the Swede was unable to race because of an injury he sustained in a crash with Ron How. During the first leg at Belle Vue, Peter was leading the deciding race when a faulty spark plug lead caused his JAP machine to grind to a disappointing halt.

Newcastle finished ninth in the Provincial League, and Brian Craven had become one of the stars and was the team's top man. He also represented a British team that was selected from the resources of the PL, and raced against an overseas side in a five-match series. He raced three times, but his best performance was 13 points in the fifth and final Test at Middlesbrough. Moreover he also raced in two matches for a Provincial League select team against a National League side. His best performance was top scoring with 12 points on his home track, although he was equally effective in his other appearance at Wolverhampton, where he finished with 10 points.

Therefore, the name of Craven was very much respected in Newcastle, and the Diamonds' supporters were thrilled to have the World Champion attend their dance at the Mayfair Ballroom. He was the guest of honour, and as such he was one of judges for the 1962 Speedway Beauty Contest — it's a hard life being the World Champion! The winner was Lynne Oliver who pocketed a cheque for £10, and a good time was experienced by all during the evening's entertainment where Peter and Brenda, Brian and Joan, were all seen displaying their skills on the dance floor.

It had been a memorable year for Peter who also finished the season as the league's top scorer. Belle Vue eventually finished in fourth place behind the winners Southampton. As well as the 'Kings of Oxford' trophy, he also won a best pairs meeting at Wimbledon with Gerry Jackson — even though he was still handicapped during the meeting. As reigning World and British Champion, Peter was at the top of his profession and was riding better than ever. But who could have predicted what was waiting around the next corner?

Six

FOREVER YOUNG

The controversial handicap system remained in place for the 1963 season, although there were some minor changes made during the winter. Midway through the season this method was coming in for some criticism from some quarters, and it was clear that some riders were having problems making their racing pay in the National League. The handicapping scheme had been looked upon as the sport's saviour when it was first introduced, mainly because there were very few riders from outside that select band of the 'Top Five,' that were able to consistently trouble this quintet.

In the *1963 Speedway Star Digest*, Eric Linden in particular seemed to be getting a little tired of their domination – particularly in the Golden Helmet British Match Race Championship. In his preview of the season he wrote, 'Can the Speedway Control Board find a match-race challenger other than Craven, Briggs, Ronnie Moore, Fundin and Knutsson, because I, for one, am sick and tired of the closed-shop stranglehold these boys have on the challenges.'

Belle Vue, of course, were led by their Wizard on wheels, Peter Craven, and Soren Sjosten returned for his second season with the Manchester team. Cyril Maidment, Jim Yacoby and Dick Fisher remained, and they were joined by Gordon McGregor, who was signed from Oxford, and a promising young find, Billy Powell.

One of the earliest fixtures was a Belle Vue *v.* Provincial League select team on 27 April. Unsurprisingly the Aces won the match 45–33, but among the opposition that evening was the New Zealander, Ivan Mauger. He had decided to return to Britain and have another crack at breaking into British racing after a less than successful spell with Wimbledon in 1958. The Kiwi joined Newcastle, where his team-mate was Peter's brother – who also appeared in this fixture.

The Provincial League riders started off the gate and the then National League riders started off 10 yards back, revealed Mauger. *I beat Peter in heat 1 in a time that was only one fifth of a second outside the track record. That one race gave me the confidence for the rest of the year, because Peter was almost beside me when we went into the first corner.*

On 20 April however, the Belle Vue crowd witnessed something that had not been seen at the track for many, many years. As the Aces saw off the challenge of Wimbledon with a 43–34 victory, Peter had crashed in heat 11. *The Ace* magazine devoted its eleventh issue to the memory of 'The Mighty Atom' in 1999, and inside it stated that it was the first time that he had fallen at Hyde Road for eleven years!

The funny thing was, during his final season, he fell off at least twice, recalled David Blinston. *I can't remember seeing him fall off at all before then. He had such balance and control. But I clearly remember that he fell heavily on the pits bend at Belle Vue in one of his last meetings before he was killed. It was a nasty fall, and although he got up almost straightaway, you could see that he was shook up – it was just very uncharacteristic of him.*

In what would prove to be his final season, Peter Craven seemed to be riding as well as ever. However, it was said that Peter wasn't very happy with the reduced number of meetings available at Belle Vue, and he was considering a move. In the issue of *Speedway Star* dated 13 April, it says that Craven wanted a move because there were only scheduled to be twenty home meetings for club riders that year. In the following week's issue, Frank Maclean reported that the Aces' management had turned down his request. Norwich were said to be keen to engage his services if he did decide to leave the famous club.

Although Peter began the season with the Aces, the transfer saga eventually went into arbitration. A court of arbitration met in London where they heard the points of view expressed by both the Aces' manager Ken Sharples, and the rider. The court then ruled that it wasn't in the best interests of speedway that PC's request for a move south was granted.

There was also talk that he had planned to make the 1963 season his final one, and one source – who was close to Peter – revealed that it was felt that he would make it his last year. After all, what was there to prove?

Talk of his possible retirement is given credibility when Brenda confirmed reports that he had been in negotiations with Charlie Oates about possibly buying his business from him. Nothing had been agreed, but it was certainly something that had progressed from beyond the idea stage. Nonetheless, if he did go ahead with buying a business, it seemed that another season would have been necessary in order to plan for his retirement. John Gibson, who was a sports journalist for the local Edinburgh paper, said that Peter had confided in him when he was in the pits during that fateful night at the Old Meadowbank Stadium that he was considering buying a motorcycle business in the Lancashire area.

Therefore, we can see that he was certainly looking beyond the glamour of the speedway track and considering his future. He even dashed from a meeting at Belle Vue to drive in the Bernie Car Rally during the night, and this fuelled more speculation about the future of the sport's most spectacular performer. The *Manchester Evening News* sports journalist, Duncan Measor, also said that Peter had confided in him that he was considering his future.

'I've always believed that you cannot mix another job with speedway, but I believe that in a year or two I will have to think about another job. I never want to go on until I am a has-been,' he told Measor.

Belle Vue were enjoying a good start to their new campaign, and by June they were sitting pretty at the top of the league. Meanwhile Peter faced Ove Fundin as the Swede's early challenger for the Golden Helmet, and despite losing the first leg at Norwich 2-1, he defeated the Swede at Belle Vue and then won the decider at Southampton to win the Helmet. Barry Briggs was no match for 'The Mighty Atom' either, as he was soundly beaten in both legs. Peter was riding like a champion, and he was rewarded with the captaincy of the Great Britain side that was due to race against the Soviet Union – except the much publicised series was cancelled!

Fundin's popularity was at an all-time low, and this was possibly illustrated to him when he met the very popular Craven in the Golden Helmet clashes. Therefore, Ernie Hancock stepped in to assist as he explained:

Ove Fundin wasn't very popular with the public outside of Norwich and Sweden. This was getting him down a bit, so I ran a 'Friends of Ove Fundin' club for him. But although I did this and I liked Ove, Peter was still my favourite. He was the best.

The first title that Peter found himself having to defend was the British Championship. He easily qualified for the semi-finals by leading the qualifiers with 43 points. He won the rounds at Oxford and Norwich with maximums. There were three semi-finals that would determine the eight qualifiers for the Final at Wembley, and the first took place at Wimbledon. PC was described in the report as 'defying the laws of balance, he was superb,' as he won with a 15-point maximum. He lost a run-off to Briggs in the second round at Southampton after they had both tied for first place with 13 points. Therefore, with the final round to go at Norwich, Peter led with 28 points while Briggs was close behind with 26. Briggs scored a maximum to win the round, while Peter finished just a point adrift with 14, which meant that on aggregate he had retained the title with 42 points to Briggs' 41. Phase one of his successful defence plan had been completed. In his column, the injured Ronnie Moore believed that Craven was riding better than ever.

Peter led Great Britain in the World Team Cup Final in Vienna, but he was far from happy on the bumpy track. Sweden won easily from

Czechoslovakia in second and Great Britain in third. Briggs scored a maximum, but his only support came from Craven who scored 8 points. Unfortunately both Dick Fisher and Peter Moore struggled to find their form. Earlier that week, PC had paired up with Fisher and won the Oceanic Trophy at Leicester while representing an England side. They finished as comfortable winners with a 6-point cushion ahead of their nearest challengers from Scandinavia, Soren Sjosten and Arne Pander.

He arrived at Wembley for his tenth World Final appearance having relinquished his Golden Helmet to his old rival Fundin. The Swede had also come in for some criticism following his win in the Internationale as an accusation of bribery was aimed at the rider who had won the meeting for the third successive year. As Ronnie Moore was injured, the winner was expected to come from the remaining quartet of Briggs, Craven, Fundin and Knutsson. Also making their debut in the Final was the Russian rider Boris Samorodov and the Norwegian Sverre Harrfeldt, who had impressed onlookers with a victory over Craven at Hyde Road.

Craven emerged for his first race in heat 2 and faced Knutsson, Peter Moore, and Peo Soderman. At the first bend it was Moore who led while PC was at the back. But he used all of his track craft to switch from the outside to the inside, and passed the Swedish duo of Knutsson and Soderman. By the end of the lap he had also slipped through on the inside of Moore, and raced away for an impressive win. It was just the start he needed as Briggs got into trouble and slid off in the next race, and left an easy win for Fundin. Luckily for Briggs, the Russian Samorodov had been excluded for clattering into England's Ron How, and he was able to remount and secure a valuable point.

Peter's second race saw him make a poor start and he was left to fight his way through to the front. But he uncharacteristically fell on the second lap and had to remount. Like Briggs before him, he was able to collect third as Per Tage Svensson of Sweden had also gone down. After all the riders had completed two races, Fundin was the only unbeaten rider on 6 points, joint second was Gote Nordin and Ron How on 5, and then came Craven, Knutsson, Briggs and Nigel Boocock with 4 points. If Peter was to maintain his grip on the World Championship then he had to win heat 9.

This time he faced Samorodov – who had already gained a dubious reputation for hard riding – Boocock, and the Welshman Leo McAuliffe. But luck just wasn't with the plucky Englishman who reared at the start, and then again as he exited the second bend. Eventually he gained control and slotted in behind Boocock, but then he unexpectedly crashed on the pits bend. The race was stopped, and Craven was excluded – his defence of the World Championship was over. He was obviously in some discomfort from a knee injury and one of the first people on the scene was Olle Nygren. It didn't look good when the medical staff carried him away from the track on a stretcher.

No one in the stadium could believe what they had seen. Most of the riders couldn't ever remember seeing Craven fall, but to see him fall twice was headline news within the sport. The contest on the track continued as Peter received some treatment in the medical room. Peter told journalist Dave Lanning:

I just gave the leg a knock and my steel shoe buckled up. When I stood up I thought I was wearing high heels or something. Now these ambulance men want to strap up the leg with sticky bandages. No fear. When I go to tear it off it will take half my leg away.

The ambulance men eventually strapped it up with crepe bandages, and Peter continued his disastrous night. He finished second behind Fundin in heat 16, and was then a distant and dejected last in his final outing in heat 19. It had been a disappointing night, but Peter wasn't the sort of man to let things like that get him down.

However, he didn't have much time to dwell on it, as he raced in the Gold Cup Final at Wimbledon where he scored 10 points, and then scored 7 points for Belle Vue as they lost at Norwich 45–33. His next meeting was scheduled for Provincial League Edinburgh.

Belle Vue had already clinched the league championship before the World Final, and it was the Aces' first league championship success since the pre-war years of 1936. Now they were hoping to achieve the double by winning the National Trophy by defeating Norwich in the final. They had won the first leg 51–33 with Craven putting in a captain's performance by scoring a paid maximum. The second leg was set for the end of September. Therefore, Edinburgh was not only welcoming the new National League champions, but also the National Trophy finalists. But, of course, there was only one Ace that the Scottish public wanted to see – and that was the double World Champion and the most spectacular rider in the world, Peter Craven.

The promoter at Edinburgh was Ian Hoskins, who was Johnnie Hoskins' son. He had revived the sport at the Old Meadowbank Stadium when he entered a team in the Provincial League in 1960. The Monarchs, as they were called, had assembled a useful side in the PL, and they were proud of their unbeaten home record that year. They had some effective riders such as Wayne Briggs, George Hunter and Doug Templeton, but for the visit of the mighty league champions from England, they strengthened their team by including Eric Boocock and Jimmy Squibb, as Briggs was unavailable due to an injury.

A visit from the glamorous club from Manchester, England, was big news in the capital city, and their team took pride of place on the front cover of the programme that evening. Hoskins had been eager to bring Craven to Scotland, as he hadn't been seen north of the border since he climbed the ladder to become his country's best rider. In his notes inside the aforementioned publication, Ian Hoskins said of Craven, 'Peter Craven is so good that until he has been seen in action he cannot be described. There are only two or three riders in the world in the same class.'

However, there were some doubts about the wisdom of Peter going to Edinburgh after two falls at Wembley – especially for an inter-league challenge match which was what can be described as a 'throw away' fixture.

Harold Jackson didn't want Peter to go to Edinburgh, revealed Alan Morrey. *He begged him not to go because he fell off at Wembley during the World Final, and he went over the high side. Normally when you do that you break your collarbone, but he didn't. So Harold thought he shouldn't go. But Peter said: 'No, I said I'd go up there for Ian Hoskins and I have never let anyone down yet.' We often wished that he did break his collarbone that night, as then he wouldn't have been able to go.*

Some 9,000 people passed through the turnstiles to see Craven's famous Aces do battle with the Monarchs from Edinburgh. The public clearly didn't see this match as a 'throw away' fixture, and it was a meeting that would live long in the memory of speedway supporters throughout the world – but for all the wrong reasons.

Peter was riding with ease, and easily won his first three races, but the Scottish club were making the most of their home track knowledge and led the Aces 34–32 as the riders prepared for heat 12. Peter was due to face George Hunter and Dudley McKean, with the young Billy Powell as his team-mate. Hunter was one of Edinburgh's top riders, and he was also earmarked for a bright future in the sport as he had qualified for the Provincial League Riders' Championship.

Peter was reportedly asked if he would demonstrate the handicap system that was in operation in the National League. He was said to have replied that he thought that the Scottish boys were going too well to be caught, but if that was what the public wanted then he was happy to start from a handicap. However, further discussions in the pits then followed.

I then made a tragic mistake, reflected Hoskins. *I asked Peter in the pits, if he would care to start 20 yards behind the other riders in his final heat of the match. As there was nothing at stake, he sportingly agreed.*

As he emerged onto the track, the crowd responded with tremendous applause. No doubt they were sensing that they would see his celebrated track craft in action, or at the very least see one of their riders lower the colours of the double World Champion. The Edinburgh riders were starting from the scratch line, and the club's number one rider, Hunter, must have sensed that he had the opportunity to claim a significant victory.

Hunter was in front coming out of the first bend, while Peter began negotiating his way through the pack – effortlessly passing his partner Powell and the other Monarchs rider, Dudley McKean – replacing Willie Templeton. He soon began closing on Hunter, and the crowd roared their encouragement to their Scottish star as the spectacular Belle Vue superstar got closer and closer with each turn. Then as the pair entered the final lap, Craven was very close behind.

The excitement in the stadium was almost at fever pitch as Hunter, sensing that his rival was close, swept into the turn. But he over-slid on the banked track and fell. Craven immediately took avoidance action and swerved to avoid him, but he was too close and his front wheel struck the back wheel of his fallen competitor and he was sent flying into the wooden safety fence.

An eerie silence fell across the stunned stadium on that September evening, as the race was immediately stopped. The various staff on duty rushed to the scene.

I was the first on the scene and I knew it was a bad one, said Leon Leat. *You get a feel for these things. When I got there, I pulled down his visor and it wasn't nice...it was a terrible night.*

Hoskins recalled:

It was so sudden, so stunning, that nobody could believe what had happened for a second or so. The impact of Craven's body against the wooden boards had been heard above the noise of the bikes. We all sensed it was serious. The ambulance officials rushed to the scene and riders swarmed out of the pits.

Among those riders that evening was Peter's team-mate, Jim Yacoby, who recollected:

It wasn't a major crash; he just tried to avoid George Hunter. I think he was putting on a bit of a show for the crowd, and I don't think Hunter had ever ridden so fast around Edinburgh! I remember I walked onto the track after the accident, and I could see that Peter was out of it [the rest of the meeting], but you're a racer and you just get on with it. We didn't know how bad it was, and it wasn't until the next day when Wilf Lucy called me that I realised how serious the crash was. I took some of his equipment back to Belle Vue after the meeting. It was a terrible loss.

Peter was unconscious when he was taken by ambulance to the Edinburgh Royal Infirmary. Hunter's mechanic informed Hoskins that his machine had seized up solid, and this was the cause of the fall. The meeting continued, and as his partner in the race, Billy Powell, explained in *The Ace* magazine, the riders just go on with it.

I recall seeing George Hunter make the gate. His bike seized and Craven swivelled to miss him and struck the fence. By this time, of course, I had gone by and I remember going straight back into the pits for the re-run. Someone told us that Peter had been taken to hospital, but in those days you just got on with things. We never really thought that much about it. Riding speedway is all about split-second stuff, and we got used to seeing riders fall off and carted away. Peter was a busy rider and we thought that he'd be okay.

It was left to Leon to make the dreaded telephone calls to his family, and arrangements were made for them to travel to Edinburgh to be at Peter's side. Charlie Oates remembered when he first heard about the crash.

I had been out to get a Vanguard as the big end had gone on it, when Brian Craven came by and he was in a terrible state. He said that Peter had had a bad accident and he needed to get up there. He also had a Vanguard but the front tyres were flat. So we borrowed tyres from the vehicle I had brought in and off he went.

Peter was in a coma at the hospital, and the surgeons became increasingly concerned as the hours and minutes ticked by. His family agonisingly waited for news, keeping a vigil at his bedside and giving him the support that he needed. The accident happened on Friday 20 September, and the days dragged by filled with stress, worry and hope. The speedway world also waited for news, as the medical staff fought to save the life of the most popular racer of his era.

Tragically, on Tuesday 24 September 1963, Peter died from the injuries he had sustained during the crash – he was just twenty-nine years old. He passed away at 9.10 p.m., and the official cause of death was given as 'severe head and brain stem injuries sustained as a result of an accident while engaged in the course of his employment as a professional speedway rider'.

Leon telephoned us about Peter's accident and we got in the car and made our way up to Edinburgh, where we stayed until he died, said Joan Craven. *Brian never got over Peter's death. It got to the point where he could hardly speak of him – it was very sad and he took it really hard. As we all did, but they were so close you see. He continued to race afterwards but it was never the same again.*

The sport was in a state of shock. *Speedway Star & News'* headlines read: 'The King is Dead – Craven was Britain's best.' It went on to pay tribute to the sport's fallen star by describing him as 'one of the greatest riders yet produced by England, will be long remembered for his unique style and brilliant balance'. The *Manchester Evening News* also paid tribute to the Aces best rider of the post-war years, and described him as 'the greatest ambassador the sport had ever known'.

Belle Vue produced a special four-page tribute that was placed inside the programmes at the club's next fixture, and it said of their fallen idol: 'There will only be one Peter Craven. He was a remarkable man and an outstandingly brilliant rider – a genius in the saddle.'

There were tributes and sympathies flooding in from around the world, but the very first telegram of condolence came from Liverpool

FC's famous manager Bill Shankly. His great friend and rival Barry Briggs said: 'Words cannot adequately express one's feelings. We've mixed it a lot, in the last couple of months particularly, at a lot of meetings. Peter was a good bloke – a fabulous rider.'

Peter Williams, like many of his colleagues, couldn't believe it when he heard the news. 'I had stopped riding in 1960, but Wilf Lucy came to tell us about Peter Craven's accident,' he recalled. 'I don't think I had seen Peter fall off once he had become a star, but I did hear that Peter had fallen off twice in the previous week. As a rider you wonder if he was tired – was it a lack of concentration? I don't remember Peter ever getting hurt.'

'I felt that it couldn't be true, because it doesn't happen to the good guys – certainly not one with his skill,' said Ove Fundin.

Peter's funeral took place at the West Derby Cemetery, Liverpool, and the service was at the West Derby Parish Church on Monday 30 September 1963. It was estimated that over forty cars made the journey to the cemetery and they received a police escort. Over 250 wreaths were sent and riders Dick Fisher and Derek Skyner were the pall-bearers along with two of Peter's personal friends. Many personalities from speedway attended, including riders, promoters and administrators – it was almost a who's who of British speedway. Among the mourners on that autumn day was Alan Morrey:

It was the biggest funeral that I have ever been to. The police put all the traffic lights on red so that the cortège could go through to the cemetery unhindered. I was stood at the graveside with Freddie Williams, it was very sad.

I was devastated, said Charlie Oates. *Even now, all these years later, I still shed a tear or two when I think of him.*

No one blamed Hunter for the crash – it was one of those unfortunate accidents that happen in speedway racing. But the young Scotsman was as shocked as everyone else, and he was very distressed about the incident.

Hunter wanted to beat Craven, said Morrey. *I think he made a point of doing that, but it was one of those accidents. It shouldn't have happened...but it did.*

Regrettably, when a tragic incident like this occurs, emotions run high. There is an emotional need to blame something, or someone, to try and make sense of it all. It is human nature. But that someone for some people was poor George Hunter.

He talked of quitting the sport, but we argued him out of it, said Hoskins. *Then the poison pen letters began arriving. We had to have Hunter's fan mail censored as they only contributed to his state of mind. There is a lunatic fringe in every sport.*

Of course George wanted to win the race, and it was true that he probably did ride that much harder than he normally would have. After all, it wasn't every day that he raced against a former World Champion at Edinburgh. The Monarchs were in the Provincial League, so they seldom came up against first class opposition. Moreover, he was young and ambitious, so of course he would try harder to win the race. But the fact of the matter was that he was in the wrong place at the wrong time.

Nonetheless, having qualified for the Provincial League Riders' Championship, the meeting was due to be staged at Belle Vue – the home of hero Peter Craven. This fixture took place just four days after he had passed away. 25,000 fans packed into the stadium to see the meeting which was won by New Zealand's Ivan Mauger, but Hunter and Ian Hoskins expected some hostility and they were not disappointed.

George and I both knew that we could be walking into trouble, recalled Hoskins. *The poison pen writers were bound to be there in strength. George even talked about pulling out, but he was persuaded to ride and do honour to Craven's memory by giving his best.*

Indeed they did receive some unfriendly chants from some sections of the crowd, but the hostilities petered out as the evening's entertainment gathered pace. George won his first four races, but an engine failure ended his challenge. When he returned to Hyde Road for the return match of the challenge, the Manchester public were more respectful to the rider – no doubt a 54–24 thrashing dished out to the Monarchs helped the Aces' fans' mood.

There was certainly no ill feeling felt by the family toward the unfortunate Hunter. Peter's brother Brian said in the tribute booklet that was published shortly after his younger brother's death:

George Hunter can't, and shouldn't have the slightest feeling of guilt in this case. Every rider – and that includes George himself – has at one time or another had to take violent evasive action to avoid a fallen rider on his bike. Only this time the consequences were more tragic. It was a thousand to one chance.

George himself hardly spoke of the incident during his career. But in 1998, he broke his silence and candidly spoke about it in an edition of *5-One* magazine. He admitted that he wanted to crawl into a hole when he met Peter's children one night in the pits, and said that he was 'frightened and embarrassed'.

I have never blamed myself because there wasn't anything I could do about it, he said. *There are many ifs and buts. If my engine hadn't blown up, it wouldn't have happened. If Peter had beaten me out of the gate, it wouldn't have happened. It was tragic because Peter was a brilliant rider and, funnily enough, I think he was the first rider I saw in action. My earliest memory of speedway is watching the World Final on a black and white television from Wembley, and Peter Craven.*

There appears to have been no major inquiry conducted into his death. However, Billy Powell recalled that he received a visit from the police the next day. He told *The Ace* magazine;

The police came round to our house and asked me to make a statement. I'd travelled back with my mate Bill Jeffs who used to help me in the pits. It was the first I knew anything was really wrong.

Peter's fatal crash at Edinburgh I think was a terrible tragedy, said Jack Fearnley. *But I can't remember any special investigation being carried out other than one which the SCB always hold after similar happenings.*

These days there would definitely have been a thorough investigation carried out by the Speedway Control Board, and it is also likely that other governing bodies would conduct an inquiry into the incident. It would appear that there could have been recommendations made about the safety of the track. Of course, one has to remember that this was forty years ago, and safety standards were not as good as they are now, but the facility did conform to the Control Board requirements of that time. However, behind the wooden safety fence at the Old Meadowbank Stadium there were heavy supporting steel stanchions, and it seems unlikely that these would pass today's health and safety regulations. Whether or not the modern paramedics of today would have been able to save the rider's life is matter for conjecture.

Such tragedies always attract controversy of one sort or another, and this one was no different. In 1997 arguments broke out in the *Vintage Speedway Magazine* about the exact happenings on that fateful night in September 1963. There were doubts cast about whether or not Peter did actually start from a handicap.

Indeed in the tribute booklet published shortly after his death, *Peter Craven – Tribute to a Great Little Champion,* its contributor, John Gibson, stated that the 'seemingly unbeatable Craven was off scratch'. The arguments were fuelled by a letter the magazine received from a reader, Dennis Anderson, who was moved to write into the publication in response to a feature written about that ill-fated evening by Ian Hoskins. He wrote that he couldn't remember Peter starting from 20 yards back, and categorically stated that Hoskins was wrong and invited the Scottish historian, Jim Henry, to confirm his version of events – Henry quoted from the tribute booklet. In his defence the former Edinburgh promoter said that he may not have been handicapped the full 20 yards – perhaps just 15 yards due to the hasty nature of the decision – but he was definitely handicapped in his last race.

Letters and correspondence flowed into the magazine's offices mainly in support of Anderson's view that there was no handicap. In fact many of the letters indicated that most of the supporters inside the stadium did not want the handicap, as they wanted to see the fast-starting Hunter and Craven begin the race on equal terms. Gibson wrote:

I asked Peter if he would follow his normal practice in the National League and start off a 20-yard handicap in his next race with Monarchs' George Hunter and Willie Templeton. 'The way these boys have been going tonight,' he said, 'I honestly doubt I could start 20 yards behind and have any chance of beating them. But if the fans want it that way it suits me.'

During the course of researching this book, I have found no concrete evidence to support either view. The match reports do not confirm one way or another. Therefore, I decided that as I wasn't present on the night in question myself, I would ask the one person who I knew was there – Peter's personal friend and mechanic for that meeting, Leon Leat.

Peter definitely started from a handicap of 20 yards, he confirmed. These people who say that he wasn't on a handicap in that race are wrong. He was chasing Hunter, who I think was riding above his ability that night and he was too close to him. When he dropped it, Peter tried to avoid him but his footrest got caught in the safety fence and he was thrown headfirst into the fence. He was too close really; if he had been a further yard or two behind him, then he'd be here with us today.

It's easy to get wrapped up in the details of the crash, but the outcome cannot be changed. That awful night was summed up by one of the track staff, Bill Campbell, who was stood about 15 yards away from the incident. He wrote from the heart in the *Vintage Speedway Magazine* and said, 'A terrible sight to witness, and a cruel loss to speedway.'

Seven

WE WILL REMEMBER

While the sport had lost one of its greatest heroes, Peter's family had lost a father and a husband. Words are not adequate to describe the utter devastation that was felt by this close-knit family, but their collective strength was invaluable during the very difficult years that followed.

My feelings about speedway were very mixed after Peter's death, Brenda admitted. On the one hand I could not help but feel resentful that speedway had taken from me my loving husband, and deprived my two young children of their father. On the other hand we had enjoyed some very happy times at speedway over the many years, and I have been left with some very happy memories.

Even though – like anyone else who is connected with speedway – I was always aware of the risks involved, strangely, I didn't really believe it could actually happen to us. I was quite unprepared for the trauma that followed. However, I was fortunate to have the love and support of all the family – without which I could not have come through it. The hundreds of letters and cards of sympathy received from speedway supporters from all over the world was also a great source of comfort.

Even though forty years have passed since Peter's death, that support from the public is still in evidence, as Joan Craven has discovered.

I think it's wonderful that people still remember Peter after forty years, and also his brother as well. There are not many people who are still remembered so fondly after all this time. Speedway was then a family sport, and I think that helps. One time, my daughter Estelle was going to Newcastle University and she had a room in the hotel. When I got there I was asked if I was related to the speedway Cravens, and I said: 'Yes, Brian was my husband.' And they replied that if they had known they would have put Estelle in the best room in the hotel! And then all the photographs came out, and it was really nice that people still remember him with such affection. Even now, incidents like that occur quite often.

The speedway bug didn't leave the family, and Peter's son Robert raced during the late Seventies for Ellesmere Port and Scunthorpe. He rode with some distinction, but the famous family name did raise expectations. A heavy crash in a second half at Swindon in 1981 left him with a shoulder injury that eventually convinced him to retire.

It's really nice that after all this time there are people who still remember my dad, for the enjoyment he gave them for a few minutes each week, and it is also gratifying that people still feel inspired to write about him, said Robert. *There is no doubt that he brought a special something to peoples' lives – he was a remarkable person both on and off the track. On a more personal note he was an incredibly loving father to both myself and Julie. I only wish we had been able to have longer with him. He always gave freely of his time for his fellow man, whoever they were, but his family was always very important to him.*

Much later after he retired from the sport, Brian became the machine examiner and the Clerk of the Course at Ellesmere Port. His son Paul also dabbled with the sport, but the dizzy heights of world stardom that Peter enjoyed did not return to the family.

British speedway, and in particular the Veteran Speedway Riders' Association have done a lot to keep Peter's memory alive. Ernie Hancock edited the tribute booklet, *Peter Craven – a Tribute to a Great Little Champion*, which was published quite soon after his death.

Don Clark ran an advert for the little book in the Sunday Pictorial, *and there were six of us in the office sending these books out to people who ordered them,* Hancock recalled. *We were able to present a cheque of £300 to Brian Craven and £200 to Brenda and the children. I have been in contact with*

Bob Andrews and Jim Courtney with regard to joining the New Zealand Veteran Riders' Association, and Jim said that he remembered me for two major contributions to the sport: the Peter Craven book and the small World Championship book that I wrote with Mike Addison and Ron Hoare.

In 1967 Belle Vue Speedway decided to honour Peter's memory by staging a Peter Craven Memorial Trophy meeting. The meeting was a prestigious individual event that was held on a regular basis, and always attracted the star names. Many of the world's top riders have won the meeting (a full list of winners is included in the back of this book), but Ivan Mauger in particular was very keen to be among the field of top riders for the first staging. He revealed:

When I heard that Belle Vue were going to run a Peter Craven Memorial Trophy, I think I was the first one to call Belle Vue and ask if I could be in the meeting. I didn't want any financial guarantees or anything – I just really wanted to ride in the Peter Craven Memorial. I put in a huge effort to win that first time, which I did, and I was very proud to receive the trophy from Brenda. I remember telling her at the time that I put in a huge effort because I didn't want to be in the meeting and get second.

Furthermore, in 1998, almost 500 riders and supporters gathered to witness the unveiling of a memorial plaque at the new Meadowbank complex which is now predominately an athletics centre. Edinburgh Monarchs supporter Allan Wilson persuaded the Edinburgh Corporation to mark the night that Peter died by having a plaque installed in the main foyer of the new stadium. The day was organised by Reg Fearman of the Veteran Speedway Riders' Association who arranged for the appearance of three former World Champions, Ove Fundin, Peter Collins and Freddie Williams.

The following year the British Speedway Promoters' Association launched a new play-off tournament at the end of the season for the Elite League. The trophy was named after Peter and called 'The Craven Shield'. Ironically, it was dropped from the calendar in 2003 in favour of another new competition called the British League Cup.

The death of Peter Craven left a massive hole in British speedway. The British supporters were lost without Peter to fly the flag in international and World Championship meetings. Riders like Nigel and Eric Boocock and Mike Broadbanks were not in the same class. Instead the British public adopted Barry Briggs as their hero, as technically he could be classed as British because New Zealand was part of the British Commonwealth.

The handicap system was abolished with the arrival of the British League in 1965, and the sport began a revival which was boosted by the emergence of new English talent such as Peter Collins, Ray Wilson, John Louis and Dave Jessup. In 1974 the successful Great Britain team was dropped, and an all-English side won the World Team Cup for the first time.

Belle Vue continued to be one of the country's leading clubs, and Peter's great rival, Ove Fundin, joined the Aces in 1967 and won the World Championship while riding for them. Then Ivan Mauger also pulled on the famous Ace of Clubs race-jacket and led the side to League Championship success. But the emergence of Peter Collins, who counted Peter Craven as a big influence on his career, seemed to represent a return to the more favourable home-grown atmosphere for the club.

He was most definitely the team's golden boy during the Seventies, and when he won the World Championship in 1976, he was England's first winner since Craven – significantly he achieved this while racing for Belle Vue. The club took a lot of pride from his victory, and it appeared to lift the grief generated by Peter's shocking death that seemed to hang over the club. Collins' victory had finally enabled the club and country to move away from the legacy of Peter Craven's achievements which, until this time, had been unmatched by another English rider.

Speedway has progressed and evolved into a very different beast to the one that Peter knew. The old World Final was scrapped in 1995, and was replaced by a Grand Prix which is now a theatre of hard, cut-throat racing, and it too is developing into a media product.

Peter's beloved Hyde Road Stadium was sold off at the end of the 1987 season for housing. It was arguably the country's best track, and yet the auctioneers coldly sold off the trophies with all the greed that was associated with that decade. The bulldozers moved in and reduced the famous old stadium to rubble. The falling timber stands creaked and cracked their protestations, and that ghostly sound played out a tearful ballad that represented the sport's breaking heart.

The Aces now race at the Greyhound Stadium at Kirkmanshulme Lane – where it all started in the 1920s – which is just a stone's throw away from the old site. But the glory days are long gone, and it has never been able to recapture the magic and the atmosphere of its old home – despite the presence of riders like Joe Screen, the Moran brothers, Jason Crump and Jason Lyons.

Craven's legacy to the sport that he graced with such style and panache is almost without parallel. It has already been said that he was ahead of his time, and his style of racing is much easier now because of the advancement in equipment and track surfaces. The photograph on the front cover of this book is an enduring image that for nearly forty years has come to epitomise the sport. The Veteran Speedway Riders' Association uses this image as part of their logo, and it is also a picture that has adorned the front of countless books and programme covers.

Sky TV now cover speedway on a regular basis, and one can only speculate just how much the producers would have loved to have a rider as charismatic and spectacular as he was. It's clear that they feel that they need a top British rider to boost their Grand Prix coverage, and one can only imagine what the ratings would have been if Peter was racing today.

I think if Peter had the equipment that they ride with today, these modern riders wouldn't know where he was coming from, said Jim Yacoby. *He was ahead of his time, because the way he rode with his balance is the way they are*

riding now. They don't put their foot down much now either. In Manchester,
to this day, everyone has heard of Peter Craven and Belle Vue speedway.

Peter was a genuine person, a gentleman, and a man among men. I don't
think anyone had a bad word to say about him, and he was a fair rider. He
wouldn't ride you into the fence or anything like that – he would always give
you room. I don't think he got the financial rewards he should have got from
Belle Vue, although he was maintained by them, by that I mean his bikes
were maintained for him there. But there was no sponsorship like that they
have today.

Of course it is very hard to compare riders of today with those that
were prominent during the 1950s and '60s. The tracks and the bikes are
much different, but natural talent always shines through and I would
like to think that he would still be a major star – just on his determination alone.

However, during 1999, *Speedway Star* and the *Vintage Speedway
Magazine* joined together to run a poll to find the supporters' best rider
of the millennium. Readers from around the world contributed their
ten best riders of all time. As a new century dawned the results were
published and, unsurprisingly, it was six-times World Champion Ivan
Mauger who came out on top. As with any poll of that nature, many
stars of the modern era found their way into the top 100 – some of
whom had yet to prove their claims to greatness. Nonetheless, in tenth
place was Peter Craven with over 2,000 points. He was beaten to the
title of 'top Brit' by Belle Vue's Peter Collins, who was one place ahead
of him in ninth place.

He was the most spectacular rider of my era, and I don't think there has ever
been anyone quite like him since he died, said Brian Crutcher. He wasn't the
best of gaters, but he would get out in the dirt and ride that line and power
around the outside of everyone. He would just turn in and go around them all.
In those days we had JAP bikes and you had to back off the power because they
were stiff to ride, so you couldn't ride them flat out like they do now. So Peter
was very unique, he would hang off the bike and peer over, or sometimes under,

those big handlebars as he would ride the boards. The only other rider who would also be slow from the start and go round everyone like that was Jack Young.
I'm afraid I thought he looked a bit scary because he was hanging off the side of his bike, recalled Ove Fundin. *But he was the only one who could do it. Some people tried to copy that style because they thought that was his secret, but no one was able to do it. There has been nobody like him. They did say that his style was because he was so small, but there have been so many other riders that have been as small as him, if not smaller, so that has nothing to do with it. He was very determined and there still hasn't been an Englishman in his class.*

There is no question that Craven was one of the sport's greats, but speedway – and motorcycle racing in general – doesn't receive either the exposure, or the plaudits, that its brave participants deserve. Is there really any other form of sport where the riders put their bodies on the line with such regularity in pursuit of championship glory?

Personally, I think it is a travesty that he was never knighted or received any such honour, said his son Robert. *He would be too modest to admit such a thing, but he was a great ambassador, not only for the sport, but also for his country too. It is my belief that he deserved some such recognition for his unsurpassed performance in the Test series in Poland alone. He was the perfect advert for what the ordinary man in the street can achieve, given the right attitude, a lot of determination and hard work.*

2003 marks the sport's 75th anniversary in Britain, and while speedway racing continues to experience both the highs and lows as every year passes by, it is comforting to know that it doesn't forget the riders who have paid the ultimate price. For as long as individuals are keen to slide motorcycles with no brakes, and the public are moved enough to watch the spectacle that it provides, the name of Peter Craven will always be written in the hearts and the minds of speedway supporters from around the world.

RACING RECORD

During the 1950s, for one reason or another, the records and heat details for domestic racing are not reliable. It is a situation that has continued to frustrate the sport's various historians. However, I am indebted to Peter Jackson for taking the time and the trouble to produce the averages below of Peter Craven's league matches. He has endeavoured to put together the most accurate averages yet devised for his league career using the now recognised formula.

Career Averages 1951-1963:

Year/ Club	Matches	Rides	Points	Bonus Points	Total Points	Cal Match Ave.	Maximums Full	Paid
1951 Liverpool	8	16	8	1	9	2.25	-	-
1952 Liverpool	5	10	5	1	6	2.40	-	-
1952 Belle Vue	4	10	3	2	5	2.00	-	-
1953 Belle Vue	12	42	70	11	81	7.71	-	1
1954 Belle Vue	24	94	194	6	200	8.51	1	1
1955 Belle Vue	24	122	256	14	270	8.85	5	1
1956 Belle Vue	22	90	194	9	203	9.02	4	1
1957 Belle Vue	19	98	269	3	272	11.10	8	3
1958 Belle Vue	16	88	239	3	242	11.00	4	3
1959 Belle Vue	15	79	212	2	214	10.84	4	2
1960 Belle Vue	16	83	217	6	223	10.75	6	2
1961 Belle Vue	18	76	201	7	208	10.95	4	2
1962 Belle Vue★	24	105	243	12	255	9.71	5	1
1963 Belle Vue★	23	94	221	17	238	10.13	4	3
Career Totals	**230**	**1007**	**2332**	**94**	**2426**	**9.63**	**45**	**20**

Calculated Match Average is the total number of points, divided by the number of rides, multiplied by four.

★ Denotes seasons when he was handicapped 20 yards.

World Championship Record:

1954	Wembley, England	3 points	15th
1955	Wembley, England	13 points	1st
1956	Wembley, England	11 points	4th
1957	Wembley, England	11 points	3rd
1958	Wembley, England	11 points	4th
1959	Wembley, England	7 points	8th
1960	Wembley, England	14 points	3rd
1961	Malmo, Sweden	6 points	10th
1962	Wembley, England	14 points	1st
1963	Wembley, England	6 points	10th

'Golden Helmet' British Match Race Championship Record:

1956

v. Ronnie Moore (Holder)	lost	0-2, 2-0, 1-2
v. Brian Crutcher (Holder)	won	0-2, 2-0, 2-0

Winter Holder: Peter Craven

1957

v. Barry Briggs (Challenger)	won	2-0, 0-2, 2-0
v. Ove Fundin (Challenger)	won	2-0, 1-2, 2-0
v. Bob Roger (Challenger)	won	0-2, 2-0, 2-1

Winter Holder: Peter Craven

1958

v. Barry Briggs (Challenger)	won	2-0, 2-0
v. Ove Fundin (Challenger)	lost	0-2, 2-0, 0-2
v. Ron How (Eliminator)	won	2-0
v. Brian Crutcher (Holder)	lost	0-2, 1-1

(Abandoned after third race due to a waterlogged track – Crutcher declared winner)
Winter Holder: Brian Crutcher

1959

    v. Ron How (Eliminator)   won 2-1

    v. Ove Fundin (Holder)   lost   1-2, 1-2

    v. Ronnie Moore (Eliminator) won 2-0

    v. Ove Fundin (Holder)   won 1-2, 2-1

    (Won by default as Fundin was unable to compete

    due to Swedish regulations)

    Winter Holder: Peter Craven

1960

    v. Ronnie Moore (Challenger)   lost   1-2, 2-0, 0-2

    Winter Holder: Ove Fundin

1961

    v. Ronnie Moore (eliminator)   won 2-0, 2-0

    v. Ove Fundin (holder)   lost   0-2, 0-2

    v. Bjorn Knutsson (eliminator) lost   0-2

    Winter Holder: Bjorn Knutsson

1962

    v. Ove Fundin (holder)   lost   1-2, 2-0*, 0-2

    *Fundin was unable to ride in the second leg due to injury

    Winter Holder: Ove Fundin

1963

    v. Ove Fundin (holder)   won 1-2, 2-0, 2-0

    v. Ove Fundin (challenger)   lost   1-2, 2-0, 0-2

Other Major Honours:

British Champion in 1962 and 1963
World Team Cup Silver Medal winner with England in 1960 and
  Great Britain in 1962
World Team Cup Bronze Medal winner with England in 1961 and
  Great Britain in 1963
National League Championship winner with Belle Vue in 1963
National Trophy winner with Belle Vue in 1958
Britannia Shield winner with Belle Vue in 1957, 1958 and 1960
Appearances for England: 50
Appearances for Great Britain: 11

Peter Craven Memorial Trophy Winners:

1967 Ivan Mauger (New Zealand)
1969 Ole Olsen (Denmark)
1970 Jim Airey (Australia)
1971 Ole Olsen (Denmark)
1974 Chris Morton (England)
1975 Chris Morton (England)
1978 Peter Collins (England)
1980 Dennis Sigalos (USA)
1985 Andy Smith (England)
1986 Chris Morton (England)
1988 Kelly Moran (USA)
1989 Shawn Moran (USA)
1990 Billy Hamill (USA)
1991 Kelly Moran (USA)
1992 Greg Hancock(USA)
1996 Jason Lyons (Australia)

BIBLIOGRAPHY

The following publications were of great use for research material:

Chronicle of the Second World War (Chronicle Communications Ltd, 1994)

Domhnulach, Alasdair, *Speedway – An introduction to the World of Oval Racing* (Empire Features, 1992)

Hoskins, Ian, *History of the Speedway Hoskins* (Vintage Speedway Magazine, 2000)

Hyam, John (Ed.), *Speedway Star Digests, 1961, 1962 & 1963*

John Chaplin's Speedway Special (Penrove Books, 1990)

Jones, Maurice, *World Speedway Final* (MacDonald & Jane's Publishers Ltd, 1979)

May, Cyril, *Ride It – The Complete Book of Speedway* (Haynes, 1976)

Mauger, Ivan, *Triple Crown Plus* (Pelham Books, 1971)

Oakes, Peter and Douglas, Peter, *The Speedway Annual No.2* (Pelham Books, 1970)

Parish Paul (Ed.), *Webster's Speedway Mirror 1972*

Robertson, Alan, *1958 Speedway Yearbook* (Privately Published)

Rogers, Martin, *The Illustrated History of Speedway* (Studio Publications, 1978)

Wick, John (Ed.), *Five Star Speedway Annual*

Williams, Andrew, *The Battle of the Atlantic* (BBC Worldwide Ltd, 2002)

Finally the speedway magazines: *Vintage Speedway Magazine, The Ace, Speedway Star, Speedway Gazette, Speedway Star* (Australia), *Speedway World* and *Speedway Weekly* (Australia).

INDEX

Index